# shadow puppets
# & shadow play

# SHADOW PUPPETS & SHADOW PLAY

David Currell

THE CROWOOD PRESS

First published in 2007 by
The Crowood Press Ltd
Ramsbury, Marlborough
Wiltshire SN8 2HR

**www.crowood.com**

This impression 2014

© David Currell 2007

**British Library Cataloguing-in-Publication Data**
A catalogue record for this book is available from the
British Library.

ISBN 978 1 86126 924 9

*Frontispiece:* **The Turkish Karagöz.**

Typeset and designed by Shane O'Dwyer,
5 Beatrice Street,
Swindon,
Wiltshire SN2 1BB

Printed and bound in Malaysia by
Times Offset (M) Sdn Bhd

# TO EMILY AND EMRE CURRELL

## ACKNOWLEDGEMENTS

In my previous books for Crowood, I acknowledged the generosity of fellow puppeteers for
their hospitality and the sharing of information about their construction methods and
presentation techniques. This is no less true of the present book for which a number of
highly regarded makers and performers have given me access to their shadow figures,
their collections and their personal archives.

I have been privileged to have had such cooperation from performers whose work I admire.
Richard Bradshaw, Ray and Joan DaSilva, Paul Doran, Jonathan Hayter, Christopher Leith
and Jane Phillips share a long and distinguished history of directing shadow play as well as
other forms of puppet theatre. All have made major contributions both directly in preparing
the book and indirectly through their work over many years. Other major influences
represented here whose past work has inspired me are Jessica Souhami, who now works
in other fields, and the late Lotte Reiniger, the silhouette film-maker whose work is heralded
as a landmark in the history of the cinema and animated film. To all these individuals my
sincere thanks are offered.

I am grateful also for information and support from Penny Francis, MBE, a tireless
advocate for puppet theatre, the Puppet Centre Trust, London, colleagues in the Design and
Technology Centre at Roehampton University, and theatrical lighting firms DHA/Rosco
Ltd. and Strand Lighting Ltd. Additional assistance with photography has been received
from Marcus Barbor, Emily Currell, Emre Currell and Jodika Patel.

## PHOTO CREDITS

Photos of Bradshaw's Shadows/Richard Bradshaw: Richard Bradshaw, except pages 183
bottom: John Delacour; 142 bottom right: Brenda Sarno; 31 bottom right, 33, 52 bottom
centre, 180: Michael Snelling; 182 top and bottom: Margaret Williams; all courtesy Richard
Bradshaw. Photos of Caricature Theatre/Jane Phillips: David Currell, except page 177,
courtesy of Jane Phillips. Photos of Compagnie Amoros et Augustin, La Citrouille, Jean Pierre
Lescot, Jessica Souhami, Teatro Gioco Vita, Théâtre-en-Ciel: Puppet Centre Trust Archive
Collection. Photo page 161: Coomber Electronic Equipment Ltd. Photos of the DaSilva Puppet
Company: David Currell, courtesy Jane Phillips, except pages 9 right: Ray DaSilva; 178: Joe
Harper, courtesy Ray and Joan DaSilva. Photos of Figure of Speech/Jonathan Hayter: David
Currell except pages: 15 bottom, 162, 166 top left, 170 bottom left and right, 179, 181 top
right: Martin Hayward-Harris; 78, 79, 103, 186 top: Stephen Holman; all courtesy Jonathan
Hayter. Photos of Christopher Leith's Shadow Show: Christopher Leith. Photos of Lotte
Reiniger's work from the author's collection: courtesy (the late) Lotte Reiniger, except pages
42 top left: David Currell; 42 top centre: David Rose; 31 top, 191 bottom left: from the DaSilva
collection, courtesy Ray and Joan DaSilva. Photos pages 136 and 157: Roscolab Ltd.
Photo of Salzburg Marionette Theatre: Gretl Aicher. Photos of Shadowstring Theatre/
Paul Doran: David Currell, courtesy Paul Doran. Photo page 25: Eugenios Spatharis. Photos
pages 152 top left, 153 top left, 159 bottom left, 160 centre right and bottom: Strand Lighting
Ltd. Photos pages 8 right, 18, 20, 96, 97 left, 132 bottom left: David Currell, courtesy Jane
Phillips. Photos pages 7, 19, 22 right, 23, 122: David Currell, courtesy Puppet Centre Trust.
Photos pages 12, 21 bottom, 26, 27, 28 top left and right, 29: DaSilva Collection, courtesy
Ray and Joan DaSilva. All other photos: David Currell, except pages: 95 bottom left: David
Rose; 41 top: (the late) Barry Smith; all from author's collection

# CONTENTS

# 1 SHADOWS AND SHADOW PUPPETS

## SHADOWS

A shadow is an image cast by an object intercepting or impeding light or the comparative darkness formed when such an object causes a difference in intensity of light on any surface. A shadow, however, does not have a separate existence but depends for its existence, its nature and its form upon the source of light that creates it and the surface upon which it is cast.

Your inseparable companion, you cannot touch your shadow nor feel it; it may be on the ground in front of you but you cannot jump over it; turn around and suddenly it is behind you; you cannot shake it off nor outrun it. Sometimes it is long and thin, sometimes shorter and fatter; sometimes it is dark and crisp, at other times faint and hazy. Shadows can appear elegant, lively, playful or grotesque, mysterious and sinister. The shadow has given inspiration to many writers, among them Edgar Allan Poe (*Shadows*), Hans Christian Andersen (*The Shadow*), Oscar Wilde (*The Fisherman and His Soul*) and Johann Wolfgang von Goethe, whose fascination with the phenomenon of coloured shadows informed his *Theory of Colour* and whose literary works used the shadow as a strong image.

Shadows have often been regarded as having magical qualities and have strong cultural, religious and scientific dimensions. Our distant ancestors had shadows from the sun during the day and from their fires at night. Their cave paintings indicate the significance of the shadow even then – this intangible, mysterious figure that undergoes transformations in its appearance and has no substance yet is visible for all to see. How were they to regard it? Was it associated with life or with death? Did it belong to this world or the next?

The shadow has been viewed at times as a disembodied spirit, a phantom or one's double and the shadow was how the ancient Egyptians envisaged the soul. Greek and Roman literature makes many references to the shadow as the soul after death and *the shades* was how they referred to hell, or Hades. In folklore only the dead, the dying or ghosts have no shadow and the Bible abounds with references to the shadow both as protective (for instance, 'under the shadow of thy wings') and as the shadow of death. Even today in Indonesia, where the shadow puppets represent ancestral spirits, gods and demons, the *dalang*, or puppeteer, still performs a semi-priestly function.

*OPPOSITE PAGE:*
*A figure from the DaSilva Puppet Company's production of Kipling's* **The Cat That Walked by Himself.**

*THIS PAGE:*
**Cinderella** *by Lotte Reiniger.*

Pliny (*Natural History, xxxv* 15) cites Egyptian and Greek myths suggesting that tracing around the outline of a person's shadow was a precursor to painting and (in *Natural History, xxxv* 43) he recounts a myth that links the shadow to the origins of sculpture. It tells of a potter's daughter who wanted to preserve the image of her lover who was travelling abroad, and so, on a wall by lamplight, she traced around the shadow of his head. The potter, Butades, used this outline to create a clay image in relief and then fired it; thus sculpture was said to have begun. Later Athenagoras draws upon the same myth to explain the origins of doll-making.

Although occasionally referred to as the poor relation of reflection, the shadow has long been a significant element in pictorial art and photography. Leonardo da Vinci identified the link between the shadow and the perception of space and many artists have suggested that the shadow is as significant as the real object, while the Surrealists use the shadow as an independent motif. In photography and film too, light and shade are essential structural elements. This is particularly evident in some of the renowned films produced around 1920 (*Dr Caligari's Cabinet, Nosferatu, The Shadow*), where shadows are used to hugely expressive effect.

The shadow is deeply imbedded in science too. As well as being used as a monitor of time, it was the shadow of the Earth on the surface of the moon that led Aristotle to deduce that the Earth is spherical and larger than the moon. The changing length of shadows led to the deduction that the Earth's axis is inclined and shadows were again used to calculate its circumference and the height of the pyramids.

These examples highlight how perceptions of the shadow have intrigued us and become woven into faiths, literature and the fabric of daily lives, providing a metaphor for human existence:

> For in and out, above, about, below,
> Life's nothing but a Magic Shadow-show,
> Played in a Box whose Candle is the Sun,
> Round which we Phantom Figures come and go.

*Edward FitzGerald (1859), translation from the twelfth-century poem,* The Rubaiyat of Omar Khayyam

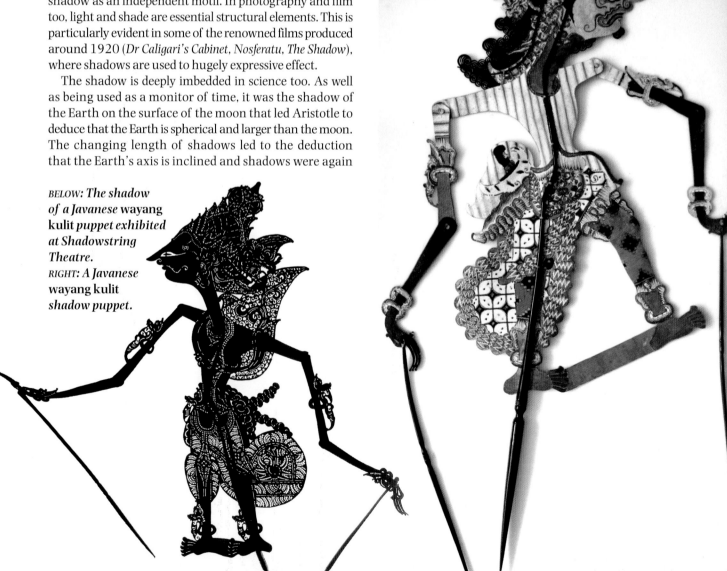

BELOW: *The shadow of a Javanese* wayang kulit *puppet exhibited at Shadowstring Theatre.*
RIGHT: *A Javanese* wayang kulit *shadow puppet.*

## THE SHADOW PUPPET

A broad definition of a traditional shadow puppet would be a two-dimensional figure held against a translucent screen and lit so that an audience on the opposite side of the screen can see the shadows thus created. However, as will be apparent in the following chapters, this has become a rather limited definition in relation to the wide spectrum of shadow theatre today.

Traditionally made of parchment or hide, shadow puppets are now usually made of strong card, thin plywood,

acetate, occasionally wire or sheet metal, but there is scope for experimentation with all manner of materials. They need not be difficult to make and can look surprisingly delicate and intricate on the screen.

When we think of shadows we tend to envisage solid black images, but shadow play often incorporates translucent figures that cast coloured shadows. The colourful, translucent, traditional Chinese 'shadow' puppets fall into this category and similar figures made with modern materials are commonly used to create colourful images. Some performers use card from which

*ABOVE: **Matsu, a figure cut in metal from lighting gobo material by DHA-Rosco for Paper Tiger, by the DaSilva Puppet Company.** LEFT: A shadow puppet cut in thin plywood by Steve and Chris Clarke (Wychwood Puppets) for Shadowstring Theatre.*

9

*An owl created in X-ray film by Paul Doran for a Shadowstring production of* Witch Is Which.

*RIGHT: **Figures created with galvanized wire.***
*BELOW: **Translucent figures created by Jessica Souhami from white card, coloured and oiled.***

shapes have been cut to project 'white shadows' and flexible, reflective surfaces are illuminated with powerful lamps to bounce light images on to shadow screens.

One should also distinguish shadows from silhouettes. The silhouette takes its name from the Marquis Etienne de Silhouette (1709–67) who was Controller-General in France in 1759. His severe measures to deal with the French economy gave rise to anything mean or cheap being referred to as *à la silhouette*. At this time black, cut-out portraits became immensely popular, particularly with the Marquis. They were so much cheaper than miniature oil paintings that they became widely known as 'silhouettes' and part of the standard French vocabulary, a term later to be adopted more widely.

*A print of an eighteenth-century silhouette chair.*

A silhouette, unlike a shadow, exists in its own right and cannot be distorted; it is an image, usually in solid black, set against a light background. So we refer to something silhouetted, not shadowed, against the light. Though not a shadow, this is a closely related phenomenon that produces similarly powerful images that can be more dramatic visually than the object itself. Olive Blackham, in *Shadow Puppets* (Barrie & Rockliff, 1960), noted this impact by highlighting the difference between the puppet placed flat on the table and the shadow it casts on the screen, suggesting that 'the strength and impact of the solid shadow is quite different from that of the object'.

In most performances the shadow puppet itself is never seen. What the audience sees is the shadow that emerges from a unique combination of the puppet's shape, the light and the screen, and for which all of these elements are essential.

The shadow-player, like a painter, is creating a picture on a surface, a picture that is then transformed by the imagination of the spectator. All puppets present an essence and an emphasis of the characters or concepts they represent and invite the audience to supply dimensions that the puppet can only hint at. In so doing, they involve the audience in a special way. This is even more true of shadow theatre where the spectator not only interprets the flat images, but also draws upon experience and imagination to give them volume and depth.

In other forms of live performance the actors inhabit three-dimensional space and are in direct contact with the audience. By contrast, shadow puppets usually have an indirect relationship with their audience, separated by a screen that filters, and sometimes modifies, the image that the audience sees.

Shadow play may present familiar objects in unfamiliar ways. It can explore an object from many angles, from a distance, in close-up, circle around it, view it from above, view it internally, show it sectioned, see right through it, or depict different views consecutively or even simultaneously. In this sense it has much in common with film. As with film, we can accelerate or slow down a process with shadow play. We can watch a flower grow and bloom or we can pause or reverse the process.

Some shadow-play traditions, such as the *Nang* in Thailand, use a static figure carved within a setting. The carving is highly suggestive of movement and this, combined with the motion of the performer who holds it aloft and the flickering live light that illuminates it, creates a sensation of movement in the shadows it creates.

*RIGHT:* **Gilgamesh** *by* Teatro Gioco Vita, *Italy.* *BELOW:* **Théâtre-en-Ciel,** *France, play with scale and show the figure sectioned with internal images.*

RIGHT: *Shadow figures used as a background to marionettes in* Eine Kleine Nachtmusik *by the Salzburg Marionette Theatre.*
BELOW: **Sunjata** *by* **Compagnie Amoros et Augustin,** *France.*

but, despite occasional flourishes of activity, it was not firmly established in its own right until the middle of the twentieth century, and even then it was very much the poor relation when compared with three-dimensional figures. It is sometimes suggested that the reason for this resides in the different cultural and spiritual mindset between east and west, that shadow play has a transcendental quality in keeping with Asian spirituality, whereas the western audience has been more comfortable with the rationality of tangible, three-dimensional representations.

In recent years, however, shadow play in Europe has undergone a revolution. The traditional performance for centuries used the rectangular screen. Even when live light gave way to electric it was comparatively basic illumination so, for clear definition, the figures had to be held tight against the screen. The figures themselves tended to be naturalistic and were used mainly to illustrate a story.

A major breakthrough came as the result of experiments in the 1960s into the physical laws ruling shadows and the appearance of the halogen lamp. Rudolf Stössel in Switzerland explored the effects of a range of materials and equipment including lenses, mirrors, prisms, foils and liquids, as well as projectors and halogen lamps. His work had a strong influence on the work of many avant-garde European companies, among them the *Compagnie Amoros et Augustin* in France and the *Teatro Gioco Vita* in Italy, who, in the 1970s, experimented further with halogen lighting and opened up a host of possibilities.

This liberated the figures which no longer needed to be held tight against the screen. The relative distances between the figure, the screen and the light could be altered to

Shadow puppets are sometimes used in conjunction with three-dimensional puppets to accompany narrated links or underwater sequences, distant action, the passage of time or as a mirror with the three-dimensional puppet in front and the shadow (or full-colour image) as the reflection. The shadow screen is aptly termed 'the cloth of dreams' in the Arab world and shadow play is particularly effective for dream sequences and memories with floating images that come in and out of focus, disappear, reappear and overlap, capturing the strange quality of this facet of human experience.

The eastern form of shadow theatre was introduced to Europe between the seventeenth and the eighteenth century

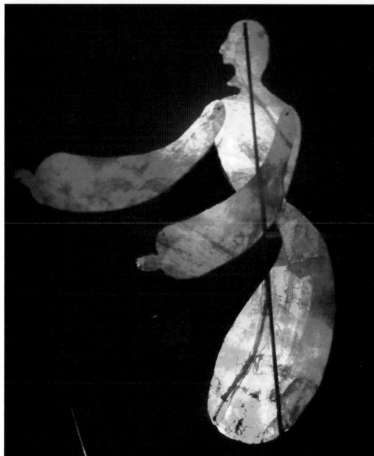

*ABOVE: **Massive projections superimposed on figures close to the screen in Gilgamesh by** Teatro Gioco Vita, **Italy.** RIGHT: **'Screaming Angel', one of a series of astral images from** Moontime **by Jonathan Hayter, Figure of Speech; the image is constructed with a collage of tissues, paint and varnish on vacforming PVC.***

change the size of the images which could fill a whole wall if required. They no longer needed a flat, rectangular screen: all manner of geometric shapes were now possible and screens could be movable. One company performed in a tent, using the whole tent as a projection surface. Rollers, castors, ropes and pulleys came into play so that screens, their shapes and their orientation could be changed during the performance. Companies explored shape, pattern, tone, line, texture and form. They experimented with the relationship between figure, screen, lighting, space and the human body, and generated new conceptions of shadow theatre.

The number of companies that perform exclusively with shadows or include shadow theatre productions in their repertoire has increased significantly in the past thirty years and shadow theatre is once again undergoing exploration by artists and giving rise to work of quality and originality.

# 2  SHADOW PLAY TRADITIONS

## ORIGINS

Some authorities deem shadow play to be the oldest form of puppet theatre. Stories regarding the origin of shadow puppets vary considerably, but they often contain common elements of death, grief or remorse, preserving through the shadow show the presence of the absent person, echoing Pliny's account of the origins of sculpture. A Chinese myth dating from 121BC tells of an emperor overcome with grief when his favourite mistress died. All attempts to ease his sorrow failed until one of the artists of the court created a shadow figure likeness of her and, after much rehearsal to capture her gestures and voice accurately, presented his shadow show with the figure illuminated behind a silk screen. The emperor was comforted and the shadow show was born.

Similarly the traditional Turkish shadow show is said to be based on real characters and features Karagöz and Hacivat, workmen engaged in building a mosque (some say a palace) in the city of Bursa during the Ottoman period. Their frequent quarrels were so amusing that other workers stopped to listen and the work was not progressing. The sultan eventually lost patience and had the quarrelsome pair executed. Later he was filled with remorse so a member of his court arranged for leather, cut-out representations of Karagöz and Hacivat to be created, to be used in shadow plays of their entertaining exploits, a tradition that survives to this day.

There is no scholarly evidence to substantiate these accounts nor others like them and some writers even suggest that string puppets appeared before shadow theatre. We also cannot be sure to what extent it was an art carried from one area to another by migration, by occupation of territory, by traders, or whether in some areas it developed quite independently.

*OPPOSITE PAGE:*
*A traditional Chinese shadow puppet made from hide.*

The similarities between the design of the traditional Javanese shadow figures and tomb representations of the Egyptian pharaohs from 3,000 years ago have tempted some to conjecture whether this might be the origin of the Javanese *wayang kulit* shadow puppets. Others draw parallels between the *wayang kulit* and the Indian *tolubommalata* puppet tradition. Although the figures themselves are quite different, scholars argue that the techniques, the repertoire, the style, conventions and rituals associated with a Javanese performance have too much similarity for India to be discounted as their origin. Certain Indonesian authorities, by contrast, hold that the shadow play techniques are of purely Indonesian origin although the themes were imported much later.

Many literary references to shadow play throughout the ages provide confirmation of its existence and lead us to believe that it was well established at the time and place that the text was written. However, they offer no further clue to its origin and, except for comparatively recent texts, little or no insight into the content of the performance, if performance is an appropriate term. An example is to be found in what is believed to be the first written reference to shadow play, Plato's *Republic*, chapter VII, 'The Allegory of the Cave', written around 366BC. It mentions figures, a fire, performing magicians, a curtain in front of the performers, an audience, and speaking and moving shadows, but nothing to support the notion of theatre, as opposed to a shadow parade. Most authorities, however, would agree that shadow play originated in the east where the ancient traditions still survive, often closely associated with religious festivals and held in higher esteem than anywhere else in the world.

## INDIA

Indian shadow figures vary greatly from region to region and different styles may be performed by different castes. Three examples of Indian shadow play are described, exemplifying both their common elements and the wide variation in the style of the puppets.

Among the most beautiful are the large, colourful *tolubommalata* puppets from the Andhra Pradesh region in south-east India. The puppets may be as much as 120 to 150cm high (48–60in) and are made from 'non-violent' hide, which means the animal died naturally. Most figures would be made from buffalo hide, though for noble figures such as a god or a king deerskin would be preferred. The hide is scraped and treated until it is stiff, strong and translucent and then coloured with dyes. Heads are generally depicted in profile and are sometimes interchangeable. The main control for a figure is a vertical, split cane with an additional cane to each hand. The legs, which are jointed at the knees, swing freely.

Traditionally, the large white screen consists of two saris extended one above the other and pinned together along the centre with date palm thorns. It can be anything up to 2m (6ft) high and 6m (20ft) wide. It is held by at least three poles, one to the top and one to each side, and often by a fourth pole along the bottom of the screen, which is about knee-high to ensure good visibility for the audience. Once

*An Indian shadow puppet.*

the only source of light was an oil lamp suspended behind and above the screen; this added charm and life to the shadows, now often created with electric lighting.

In keeping with other eastern traditions and the common theme of the struggle between good and evil that runs through these stories, the figures are divided on each side of the screen with noble, virtuous characters to the right and evil characters to the left, as viewed from backstage.

A performance often begins mid-evening and continues throughout the night, the puppets performing to an accompaniment of songs and narration. Music is a significant element of a performance and is provided by a harmonium, drums and cymbals. The performers stand behind the screen to operate the puppets; they wear ankle bells and provide both rhythm and sound effects by stamping their feet on two wooden planks placed one on top of the other. Male and female performers speak for male and female figures; in the past, only men operated the puppets but now women are involved in the manipulation too. The performances have religious significance as well as being entertainment: they are often given in temple grounds as part of a temple festival and may be intended to appease the rain gods and to promote the welfare of the animals. Frequently the performance will open with a religious ritual such as a prayer of supplication to Lord Ganapathi. The stories are based upon the Hindu epic poems, the *Mahabharata* and the *Ramayana*, interspersed with local gossip and topical commentary that provide light relief.

*Ramayana* means 'life of Rama' and favourite stories tell of Rama's marriage to Sita, their banishment to the forest with his brother Laksmana, Sita's abduction by the monster king Rahwana and her rescue with the help of the monkey king Hanuman, after numerous battles. The *Mahabharata* deals with the conflict between two branches of a family descended from the supreme gods of Hinduism. One branch usurps the throne from the rightful heirs, causing a dispute that can be resolved only by war that involves several generations of the family. It is finally settled with a victory for justice and the concept of right. Everyone knows the stories well, so, during the performance, members of the audience may come and go, eat their meals and so on. At some point the performer makes a collection and, if anyone refuses to contribute, he is ridiculed by a comic puppet character that utters obscenities and makes vulgar gestures at him. Oral tradition dates the *tolubommalata* back to at least 200BC and there is some documentary evidence that may be interpreted as indicating shadow play somewhat earlier than this.

A marked contrast to the *tolubommalata* puppets is to be found on the east coast of India north of Andhra Pradesh in Orissa. Here shadow play is known as *ravanachhaya* (the shadow of Ravana) and the performers are traditionally descendants of musicians and officials of the local royal court. There are similar themes, taken from the *Ramayana*, and similar musical accompaniment, but the figures are small, unjointed and perform with simple movements. Deerskin is used for divine characters while other figures are made from sheepskin or the hide of mountain goats; the hide is not scraped so thoroughly as that of the *tolubommalata* puppets and so it is thicker and opaque. The puppets have quite a detailed outline and expressive poses but they have little internal, cut-out ornamentation.

In the Kerala region on the south-western coast, shadow play is known as *tolpavakuthu* and similarly tells stories taken from the life of Rama. It has some features in common with the style in Orissa, including musical accompaniment with percussion instruments, but the performances are generally given by scholars or poets who recite both prose and verse in a stylized fashion. Rituals feature in the performances, often performed in temple grounds as part of religious festivals. The puppets are traditionally made entirely of opaque deerskin and range from approximately 50 to 80cm high (20–30in). Despite the modest size of the puppets, the shadow screen may be anything up to 12m (39ft) wide, with some 130 figures operated by at least five puppeteers.

# INDONESIA

Puppet theatre in Indonesia, particularly in Java and Bali, is an important part of the culture and no type is more so than the *wayang kulit* shadow puppets. *Wayang kulit* has a number of forms each of which draws upon a distinct repertoire, but the best known is *wayang purwa* which takes its themes from the *Ramayana* and the *Mahabharata*. It is so much a part of Javanese life that even shop signs and business logos feature major shadow characters. The term *wayang* is a general one referring to the theatrical

*Indian shadow figures.*

19

performance and is said by some to refer to the concept that all art is a shadow of life; it is qualified further by terms that define the type of puppet, *kulit* being hide and *purwa* meaning ancient.

The shadow puppets are the most common of all the *wayang* figures and it is widely held that all forms of Javanese theatre originated from the shadow play. The puppets are about 60cm (24in) high and usually made from buffalo hide treated to produce parchment. The process involves the removal of excess oils, sun-drying, smoothing, soaking, stretching, drying, scraping, rubbing and polishing. When the parchment is ready, the separate parts are cut out and the delicate, filigree-type pattern is chiselled into each. The

*A Javanese* wayang kulit *shadow puppet.*

eye is the last feature to be cut since it is believed that this is when the puppet's life begins.

The process of carving the skin and the design of the figures is set down by tradition and is related to the character portrayed. As soon as a puppet enters, its appearance conveys to the audience its rank, its character and, in fact, almost all they need to know about it. In addition to the profile shape, the decorative headdress and other adornments, information is conveyed by the eyes, by the angle of the head and even the distance between the feet. Virtuous, noble characters will have refined features, almond-shaped eyes and graceful bodily shapes with the head tilted slightly forwards, while crude characters will have larger bodies, round eyes, bulbous noses, pointed teeth and feet set wide apart in a fighting stance.

The figures are generally opaque when decorated; despite being used for shadow play, they are painted and gilded in a highly ornate fashion since the audience may watch not only their shadows but the actual figures behind the screen. At one time women were restricted to watching only the shadows while men were permitted to watch both the shadows and the actual puppets, which include representations of gods, demons and ancestral spirits.

Facial colouring varies with an individual's character and a number of versions of a figure may be used with different colourings during a performance to indicate changes to its character or personality over time. Black is associated with virtue and wisdom, white with youth and beauty, gold also suggests beauty (or sometimes is simply used as decoration without any connotation), blue denotes cowardice and red suggests aggression and untrustworthiness.

Three control rods are used, traditionally made of horn with the main vertical rod shaped to follow the line of the puppet's design and tapered to a point at the base. The arms are jointed at the shoulder and elbow and the hands are attached to controls, but the legs are carved as part of the main figure and not jointed.

Unlike the Indian figures that may be operated by a group of standing or dancing performers, *wayang kulit* performances have a single puppeteer, the *dalang*, who sits behind his screen to manipulate the puppets, providing narration, speaking all the dialogue, conducting the *gamelan* orchestra that sits behind him, and sometimes singing too. He sits and performs from dusk to sunrise without a break and, between the toes of his right foot, holds the *kechrek*, a kind of rattle or mallet which he strikes repeatedly against a wooden box in which the puppets are stored when not being used. A system of

*The differences in* **wayang kulit** *designs are highly significant, indicating both rank and personality; the hide is treated to become parchment, which, unlike leather, is translucent unless it is painted or gilded.*

*Lotte Reiniger's scraperboard impression of a* **wayang kulit** *performance, with the gamelan orchestra sitting behind the* **dalang,** *who performs with an oil lamp suspended above him.*

21

signals indicates his intentions to the orchestra almost imperceptibly.

The role of a *dalang* has been likened to that of a priest; not only is he a regular feature of festive and ceremonial occasions, births and marriages, but, as the puppets are considered to be the incarnation of ancestral spirits, the *dalang* acts as a medium between the spirits and his audience. Clearly, whoever becomes a *dalang* must have an array of personal qualities far beyond that of entertainer and he is thus a highly respected artist.

The screen, or *kelir*, is approximately 1.5m high and 4.5m wide (5ft×15ft). Made of cotton, it is supported by bamboo sticks with the base at, or near, ground level. Two long stems of banana plants are placed along the bottom of the screen and the sharp, pointed ends of the main control rods are plunged into the stems to hold the puppets securely when they are off stage, the good characters on the right and the evil on the left, from the puppeteer's perspective. With the puppets arrayed in this way, the space between them, which represents the stage, is about 2m wide.

Before the performance, the *gunungan*, which represents a mountain or a tree, stands in the centre of the stage; the *dalang* removes this from the screen to signal the start of the performance. Although Java is now mainly Islamic, the plays continue to draw upon the Hindu epic poems, which were introduced to Java from India about 2,000 years ago. However, the stories, numbering about 200, have undergone many changes to both their names and content and now have a distinctly Javanese flavour. They reflect Javanese attitudes and values and are very much part of Javanese culture and its national heritage.

Traditionally, a single oil lamp was hung above and behind the screen as the sole source of illumination and this flickering light, coupled with the beautiful figures and the *gamelan* music, created an amazing, almost hypnotic effect.

## THAILAND

Shadow theatre in Thailand is also said to have originated in India and includes the *nang talung* puppets which are similar in form to the *wayang kulit* and still to be seen, and the *nang yai*, which is very different from the examples described earlier and now rarely if ever seen. Essentially a form of folk theatre, the *nang yai* figures depicted an entire scene rather than individual characters. They were made from cow or buffalo hide and treated in a similar way to the Javanese figures before their construction.

The character and the scene in which it is set was cut in one large piece of hide, which could be as much as 2m high and 1.2m wide (7ft×4ft). Sometimes figures were coloured for use in daytime performances while plain figures were used for performances at night. Each figure

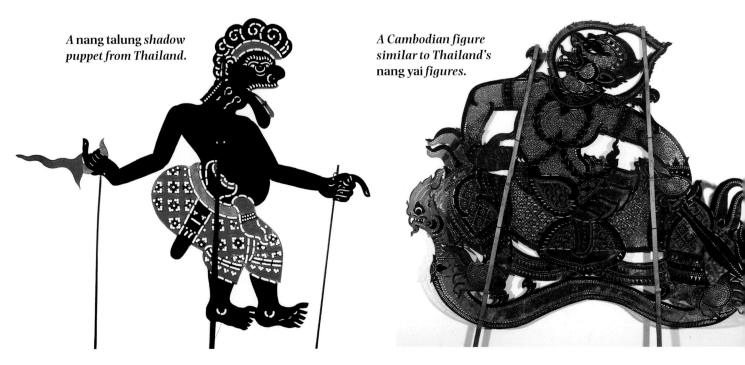

*A* nang talung *shadow puppet from Thailand.*

*A Cambodian figure similar to Thailand's* nang yai *figures.*

was supported by two long sticks which the performer held aloft, most frequently in front of the large white screen, taking it behind the screen to cast shadows by firelight to suggest action at a great distance. In order to contain such large figures the screen was up to 12m long and over 4m high (40ft×14ft). The performer's dancing movements, resembling the *Khon* classical dance, coupled with the flickering light of the fire and the design of the figure all contributed to give life to the static images.

The performances, based upon Thai dance dramas of the *Ramakien* (the Thai *Ramayana*), were presented with narration accompanied by percussion and stringed instruments. Performance styles similar to the *nang talung* and the *nang yai* are to be found in Cambodia and in other parts of the east, but the *nang yai* type of performance is less common than those that use individual puppet figures.

# CHINA

It is widely held that shadow play in China dates back at least 2,000 years and possibly much earlier, but the first written or pictorial evidence found dates from the Sung dynasty (AD960–1279). Writers suggest that it reached its height of artistry in the eleventh century and that this is the origin of the shadow play in the Middle East, introduced by Mongols in the thirteenth century. Indeed, some suggest that here lie the origins of shadow play throughout the east, if not the world.

The traditional Chinese shadow play is stylized, containing romance, heroic adventure, fantasy and humour. The shadow puppets are usually quite small,

delicate and elaborately decorated. There are two types of traditional figure which are distinguished by their size, method of construction and the positioning of the control rods. The Peking (northern) shadow puppets are just over 30cm (12in) high and intricately made from the belly of a donkey. The hide is treated to make it translucent and then brightly coloured with dyes. The Cantonese (southern) figures are larger and of thicker skin so that they cast a more solid shadow.

Each figure has three controls consisting of wires that are fastened in rods, the main supporting control and a

*ABOVE: **Old Chinese human figures; the controls would be fixed into wooden rods.***
*BELOW: **Old Chinese animal figures.***

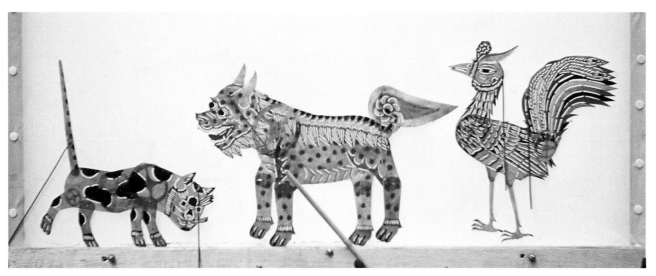

control to each hand or arm; the legs hang freely. The main rod on the Cantonese figures is attached at right angles to the head so it is less visible on the screen. The main supporting rod on the Peking figures is held parallel to the body and the top of the wire is bent at a right angle to attach it to a hide collar at the puppet's neck. The collar is used because the heads are often interchangeable so that several heads may be used with one body. These rods are more visible on the screen but they are clear of the puppet's shadow.

The heads have to be readily distinguishable; the faces are stylized, always depicted in profile, and those of rulers, heroes and women are heavily cut away, leaving only a very thin outline. Bodies are created in different ranks so that any head of a certain rank may be easily matched with an appropriate body. Arms and legs are articulated and sometimes there are also wrist joints. Traditionally, the heads were always removed at night because of the ancient belief that otherwise the puppets would then come to life. The figures were stored in a muslin book or a box lined with fabric and some puppeteers even took the precaution of storing heads and bodies in different books.

The shadow screen, made of white translucent cloth, is approximately 1.5m wide and 1m high (5ft×3ft). It is

*The Turkish Hacivat and Karagöz.*

supported by a bamboo framework with bright drapes surrounding the screen. Scenery tends to be simple and symbolic and, as elsewhere, traditional lanterns have increasingly given way to electric lighting for illumination.

## TURKEY

Many scholars consider the origins of shadow play in Turkey to reside in Indonesia but some authorities advance the theory that shadow players were introduced to Turkey from Egypt by Yavuz Sultan Selim, who conquered Egypt in 1517. Yet another theory suggests that the popular Turkish shadow show featuring Karagöz and Hacivat originated in the fourteenth century. Certainly Karagöz is regarded by many as the most important entertainment of the Ottoman period. It was played throughout Ramadan, during other festivals and special occasions and appeared in coffee houses and public gardens. The performances reflected the culture of Istanbul whence it was spread to other parts of Anatolia by travelling performers, possibly reaching its peak of popularity in the eighteenth century. The name Karagöz is a compound of *kara*, meaning black, and *göz*, meaning eye, for he is always depicted with one dark eye.

A tradition that survives to this day, Karagöz is a popular, witty, folk hero who has always commented on social events and poked fun at authority with a knockabout style of comedy combining satire and irony, clever plays on words, double meanings and exaggerations. Some commentators suggest that there are also elements of philosophy and Islamic mysticism, the other main character being Hacivat, who, in contrast to Karagöz, is educated in Islamic theology. The performances conclude with an apology to the audience for any errors made during the show. There is also said to be an extinct form of Karagöz play, known as Şekerli Karagöz (Sweet Karagöz), or Toramanlı Karagöz (meaning young, wild or untamed), in which the language was coarse and vulgar. Female characters were naked and Karagöz, depicted with a phallus, performed graphically explicit sexual acts on women and young boys.

The puppets are jointed, between 30 and 40cm high (12–16in), and generally made from camel or cow hide which has been treated to make it translucent. Some accounts suggest that the very first figures were made from leather slippers. Details are cut with sharp blades and colour is added with Indian inks or natural dyes.

The name for the screen, which is held by a wooden frame, actually means 'mirror'. At one time it was 2.5m wide by 2m high (8ft×6ft), but now it is often scaled down to less than half this size. Scenery is depicted by cut-out sets placed to the sides of the screen and easily interchanged. Behind and below the screen is a wooden ledge on which are placed instruments such as cymbals, a tambourine and pipes; the ledge is also used to hold a string of electric lights, which have replaced the traditional lantern. The closeness of the lights to the screen renders the horizontal control rods very faint, if not invisible, but causes the shadows to fade from view if the puppets are moved only slightly away from the screen. The performances are given by a single player who may sometimes have an apprentice or assistant. The puppeteer operates all the characters, speaks for them in a variety of dialects, for many ethnic groups are represented, and chants or sings songs too.

Today, live Karagöz performances are not so common but are most often seen in tourist hotels and restaurants. It, however, frequently appears in cartoon format on Turkish television. A fascinating feature of the televised Karagöz cartoons is the way in which they have remained true to the idiosyncrasies of shadow play. When other popular images are made into cartoons, they usually adopt the conventions of cartoon film, making all manner of actions or incredible events possible, but, in this instance, the figures retain the characteristics of shadow puppets. For example, they continue to move in the somewhat jerky fashion of the live puppets and they exit backwards because the puppets cannot turn around. In this way the Karagöz cartoons come as close to the live show as it is possible to be.

## GREECE

There are many conflicting theories of the origins of the Greek Karaghiosis shadow play that closely resembles the Turkish Karagöz. Some suggest that it was carried from China by Greek merchants, others that it was invented by a Greek during Ottoman rule; the legend of Karagöz and Hacivat working in Bursa is also offered as another explanation. It is quite widely held that it actually came to Greece from Turkey in the nineteenth century and that a significant element in its appeal at that time was the character's large phallus and its obscene actions and language. The character has since become adapted and integrated into Greek culture as a firm part of folklore. The Greek version is poor, barefoot and hunchbacked with tattered clothes. His right arm is always shown as very long, usually with several joints. He lives in a modest cottage with his wife and children and devises a host of

mischievous ways to obtain money and feed his family. He is a liar, sometimes violent, yet good hearted and faithful. There appear to be two types of Karaghiosis play, the comical type and that known as 'heroic', set in Ottoman times, in which Karaghiosis appears as the assistant of an important hero.

Puppeteers do devise their own original stories, but there are many handed down by oral tradition and played according to a conventional formula with only minor variations among performers. Students of other forms of puppet theatre will see the many similarities that exist between this Greek or Turkish tradition and the western figure of Punch, another anti-hero who pokes fun at authority and is depicted with a hunchback and a stick that has replaced the original phallus. He too is violent, a liar with mischievous qualities and originally there were some crude aspects to his performance, which has also been handed down largely by oral tradition.

The puppets are created and presented in much the same way as their Turkish counterparts. They are made from camel skin and always shown in profile. Many of the characters have simple joints while two have neck joints and an articulated head. Most of the puppets are operated

*Hatziavatis and scenery from the Greek version of* **Karaghiosis.**

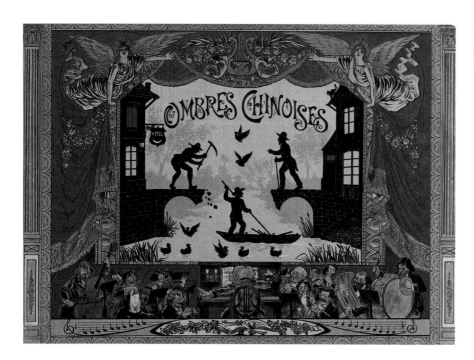

**Ombres Chinoises:** *a French proscenium and performance of* **Le Pont Cassé** *(The Broken Bridge).*

by a single horizontal rod, though Karaghiosis and a few others require hand controls too. Traditionally, the scenery consists of his cottage at one end of the screen and the vizier's palace at the other.

During the 1980s Karaghiosis performances were televised weekly, either as live shows with an audience or pre-recorded with special effects. They included a mix of themes from Greek myths to modern items such as trips into space. Now live shows are less common, Karaghiosis appearing mainly at festivals or folk events. The name is also now taken to mean 'joker' and is used as an insult.

## WESTERN SHADOW THEATRE

Early puppet theatre in Europe did not enjoy the attention of artists, poets and playwrights in the way or to the extent that it did in the Far East and the Ottoman empire. In Europe, puppetry in general appears to have remained largely the province of wandering showmen for a considerable period, but shadow play was certainly known in Elizabethan England. In Ben Jonson's *A Tale of a Tub* (1633) shadow figures of the actors in the play re-enact the play they have performed and the screen is referred to as 'a fine oiled lanthorn [lantern] paper that we use'. Early shadow theatres almost certainly had a narrator who stood beyond the stage in view of the audience and explained the action while the puppets acted only in pantomime and spoke no

dialogue. This was common in other forms of puppet theatre throughout Europe and 'the interpreter of puppets' is frequently referred to in England in Elizabethan times.

During the second half of the eighteenth century a form of shadow play known as *Ombres Chinoises* became popular. It is thought to have been introduced in Italy and Germany, then France where the name was acquired, and then was brought to England. There is no actual record of who introduced it to Europe, although it is said to have been carried by sea from China. At first, the figures were small, black cut-outs that bore more resemblance to fashionable silhouettes than to their Chinese predecessors. They were made of solid, black card or pasteboard, were operated by rods or pegs and were technically quite sophisticated.

The first mention of these performances was in 1760 when a showman named Audinot exhibited at the Foire St Germain in Paris. An Italian who adopted the French name Ambroise is also recorded as giving shadow shows, first in Paris in 1772 and then in England in 1775. These are the first known public shows of this kind in England. Presented by English, French and Italian performers, the *Ombres Chinoises* became a fashionable entertainment with similar repertoires that usually included a performance of *Le Pont Cassé (The Broken Bridge)*, the best known of all the shadow plays. Strictly, it was not a play but a humorous song with a refrain and it was so popular that it continued to be performed for over a century.

DE CHINEESCHE SCHIMMEN.

*Two further prints showing performances of* The Broken Bridge, *one of uncertain origin, the other Dutch.*

In 1776, Dominique Seraphin opened an *Ombres Chinoises* theatre in Paris, five years later moving it to Versailles, where it was a great success with the nobility. He returned to Paris in 1784 and the bourgeois flocked to see his shows, but, it appears, not the common working people. After briefly parting with the theatre, Seraphin bought it back and continued to perform (now including marionettes) until his death in 1800; family members maintained the theatre for a further seventy years.

The popularity of shadow play declined towards the end of the eighteenth century but rose again in England around 1835 with the appearance of the 'galanty' shows. After dark, the Punch and Judy showmen would secure a screen across the proscenium opening of their booth and perform shadow shows by candle light. This was sometimes a risky business in windy conditions or if they became the victims of young hooligans who would delight in rolling the booth. *The Broken Bridge* continued to be the most popular item throughout the galanty era. Henry Mayhew in *London Labour and the London Poor*, vol. III (1851) includes a section on street entertainers which contains a wonderfully colourful account of the Punch and Judy man, galanty shows, and the paper profile cutter, told in the words of those he interviewed.

In Victorian Britain, publishers of the Toy Theatre (or Juvenile Drama) sheets known as 'penny plain, twopence

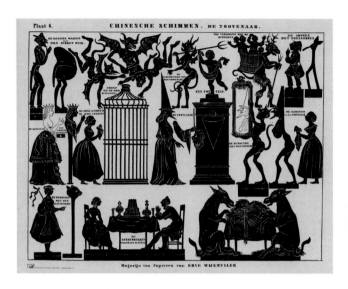

*ABOVE: Examples of Dutch and German sheets of* Ombres Chinoises *figures.*

*A print from an original woodcut for an English harlequinade.*

coloured' adopted a practice already well established in France and elsewhere in Europe and produced sheets of black and white figures, 10–15cm (4–6in) high, to cut out and mount for shadow play. The French publisher Pellerin also produced a sheet of transformation figures not so different from those described in the chapter on detail, decoration and transformation. The printing of these French sheets of shadow plays ceased in 1914.

In Britain, magazines for juveniles, such as *The Boy's Own Paper* in 1882, would sometimes carry descriptions of how to make a shadow show and *The Boy's Own Book* of 1880 actually gave instructions for creating multiple shadow images by moving a number of lighted candles behind a figure suspended on thread, which is an effect that contemporary shadow players still explore. At that time many families created their own shadow shows in their homes until the introduction of the magic lantern, though some of the early magic lantern slides projected moving shadows and the magic lantern was also used at times to project scenes for use with shadow puppets.

Meanwhile, in Paris in 1862 artists, writers, poets and musicians of note combined with prominent government figures to create the tiny *Theatron Erotikon de la Rue de la Sante* in which they presented performances in an auditorium which could seat only twenty-one people. This theatre closed after a year but it had proved so entertaining that the idea spread to cafés and cabarets, one of the most successful being *Le Chat Noir* café-club of Rodolphe Salis in the Rue Victor Massé in the Montmartre district. On one occasion

LE CHAT NOIR *CLUB IN PARIS.*

*ABOVE: **The exterior of the club.***
*RIGHT: **Backstage during a performance.***

*LEFT: **The audience and the shadow screen.***
*BELOW: **Shadow figures from the** Chat Noir.*

a small hand puppet booth was converted into a shadow stage by the painter Henri Rivière, who fixed a white napkin into the proscenium opening against which to perform with small, cut-out figures. Rivière subsequently became the guiding light of the club, transformed it into a proper theatre and involved members of his staff, including the cartoonist Caran d'Ache who experimented with perspective and depth. They constructed a larger fixed screen, cut figures up to 45cm (18in) high from zinc sheets, introduced colour and even projected sets with arc lights. Over a ten-year period they created more than forty productions, described as masterpieces with poetic, satirical and humorous content.

In 1896 *Le Chat Noir* played the shadow shows for the last time and the following year, after the death of Salis, the cabaret closed down, having given inspiration for other shadow theatres that continued to perform for some years.

The shadow play tradition continued into and throughout the twentieth century. In the 1920s the animated, silhouette films of Lotte Reiniger first appeared in Germany (*see* the chapter on silhouette films, page 191).

Later transferring to Britain for much of her career and working also in Canada, her impressive list of film credits drew upon themes ranging from fairytales to the *Tales of the Arabian Nights* (*The Adventures of Prince Achmed*) and to Mozart (*Papageno* was one of many). These films, together with her demonstrations and her figures and sets for live performance, had an important influence on both animation and shadow theatre.

There were other significant individual exponents of the art in eastern and western Europe and work of considerable vitality appeared between the 1940s and 1960s, shadow play now becoming more widely recognized and explored. The developments in the 1970s, noted in the first chapter, have continued to extend the boundaries of the art.

In the twenty-first century there are many fine companies and individuals, some represented in this book, which either specialize in shadow play or include it in their repertoire. Some are preserving the traditional forms of shadow play of great charm and poetic quality while others are challenging popular conceptions of shadow theatre and exploring its possibilities in new and exciting ways.

*Mozart's* The Magic Flute, *a silhouette film by Lotte Reiniger.*

ABOVE: *A cut-out design in paper on card for* The Happy Prince, *created by Lotte Reiniger for the Hogarth Puppets.*

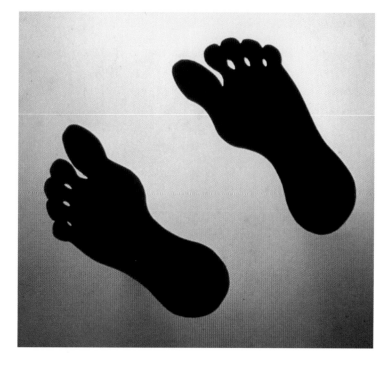

ABOVE: *Tchi-Tchi by Richard Bradshaw, Australia, who is widely regarded as the finest solo shadow player in the world; the puppet's eyes move and the expression changes as it speaks directly to the audience and sings.*
RIGHT: *Two feet from a sequence of feet, some of which move strangely or transform, by Bradshaw's Shadows.*

# 3 SHADOW PUPPET DESIGN

## BASIC CONSIDERATIONS

Before you embark upon the design of the figures and sets for your chosen performance, there are some fundamental aspects to be considered. Most of these are interdependent, so each decision you make about some aspect of the action, puppet construction, control, staging or lighting will have implications for each of the others.

What atmosphere or general effect do you wish to create? What types of figure are in keeping with the piece to be played – opaque or translucent, solid or with cut-out detail, plain black, partly coloured or full colour, and in what style? Some designers determine a particular artistic style for a production, as this provides a unifying framework. Their inspiration may be anything from primitive or native art to stained glass windows or surrealism. What characters are required and how many operators will there be? This has implications for how many figures an operator might

need to handle at a particular moment and, if more than one, what controls a figure can usefully have. Do you need multiple versions of a character, possibly with different jointing, to achieve different actions or to appear in different costumes? What method of control is appropriate? This will be determined partly by your own preference but in large part by the size and the nature of the puppets and what the action, the type of lighting and the stage design requires.

Decisions about the size of the puppets, how they are to be used and the size, shape and number of screens go hand in hand and must take account of the potential size of any audience, as well as the fact that small puppets will be lost on a large screen. The number of figures present in any one scene is another factor that influences the relative sizes of screen and puppets. It also determines the number of operators required who must be accommodated behind the screen: the puppets may fit on the screen but will the operators fit behind it too?

*OPPOSITE PAGE:*
*Shiva from* Rama, *a multi-media shadow show combining animation, original music and live puppetry by Figure of Speech.*

*THIS PAGE:*
A Tale of Two Fishes, *by Richard Bradshaw, deals with prejudice and integration.*

**Machins, Machines et Compagnies** *by* La Citrouille, *France.*

How many scenes and scene changes are required? What scenery is needed and how can this be portrayed effectively without unduly restricting the acting area?

The design concept for the performance includes the staging structure, operating positions and the method and positioning of lighting, which once again are interrelated. For example, if you are using projectors, you cannot operate a figure for which the method of control requires you to stand immediately behind it, so you need to reconsider either the method of control or how you intend to light the production. The light and the screen are no longer regarded as passive elements of a performance but may be manipulated to convey atmosphere or to create a setting that evolves with the performance. This presents many possibilities for combining and manipulating puppet, screen, light and sometimes actors too.

If you are to take your show to your audience rather than have the audience come to you, you must consider how you are going to pack it securely and safely, which might increase the weight, and how you are going to transport it. Will the staging fit the available transport? Does it need to be designed in smaller sections to be assembled at the venue? How will this affect setting-up time? Will the staging suit different venues? What will be the minimal requirements of your proposed production in terms of stage dimensions, height availability, blackout conditions and availability of power supply? It is quite likely that you will modify some aspects of the performance at each stage in its development in order to achieve your objectives.

## SHADOW PUPPET STRUCTURE

Shadow puppet design requires you to create figures that convey the characters or ideas you intend, that move in keeping with their characteristics and that are not too complicated to operate.

Simple, non-articulated shapes can be used and are appropriate for early explorations by children. In adult productions they tend to be used for groups of figures or processions, for songs and dances, for a particular effect or design concept, or with forms of lighting and associated techniques that give life and apparent movement to the figures. Even the slightest movement is an improvement on rigid figures and you might achieve this simply through the addition of suitable fabrics or trimmings.

It is more common for shadow figures to be articulated in some way. The joints may follow the main points of articulation of a human or animal figure or might depart from these to achieve the desired movement. Head, neck and body may be a single piece or may be jointed either at the base of the neck alone or where the neck joins both head and body. If you articulate the head, you will need either to attach the main control to it or to have one control to the head and another to the body, though additional controls are not required for all the articulated parts of a figure.

Arms are usually jointed at the shoulder, but might or might not have elbow or wrist joints, so the arm may be cut in a fixed position. Sometimes one arm is articulated and

*ABOVE AND RIGHT:* **The aeroplane and businessman are examples of simple, non-articulated shapes.**

*BELOW:* **Articulated figures by La Citrouille, France.**

*Three different hip joints based on designs by Richard Bradshaw: the legs are joined at separate points on the body, at the same point on the body, or one leg is joined to the body and the other leg to the first leg's thigh.*

controlled while the other swings freely or the second arm might not be articulated at all but in a fixed position. An arm might be cut together with the head, neck and shoulder as a single unit that is pivoted on the body at the top of the arm, so the head and the arm move together.

Legs usually swing from the hips; they might have knee joints but rarely have ankle joints since the toes will tend to drop downwards. Occasionally, rather than attach both legs to the hips, which is normal practice, one leg might be attached in this way but the other be made somewhat shorter and suspended from the other leg's thigh instead. This is not widespread practice but an example of a solution to a particular design requirement. It is all about adopting whatever method works.

A body might have a joint at the waist or it might be designed in several parts which, when joined together, give greater flexibility and variety of movement. This principle has wider application too; for example, you might make an arm in several jointed parts. Moving mouths are best

*Horus, an acrylic figure designed in Egyptian style by Jonathan Hayter; the clear waist joint (LEFT) is a feature of the visual design as well as giving greater flexibility of movement.*

avoided unless they are absolutely essential. They are most frequently used for comic effect, sometimes projected with a very large image. The attempt to synchronize the moving mouth to speech is not recommended. With shadows in particular it is difficult to achieve this convincingly and it can be boring to watch because the undue attention this requires from the operator can detract from the other movements of the figure. (Having said this, I am now sure to come across an example that contradicts this view, but that's shadow puppetry!)

Remember the effects of gravity on any moving part when the figure is held up to the screen. What looks good on your design and moves well when placed flat on your work surface might not appear the same on the screen. A fully jointed arm might hang down limply if it is not specifically controlled, or it might swing to good effect, possibly depending on where it is joined to the body. On the other hand, an arm designed in an interesting position with no elbow or wrist joint might sit and swing naturally in a more interesting way, depending on where it is joined to the body and how it is balanced. Often the only way to tell is by experiment.

Sometimes the design of the puppets requires a good deal of trial and error, exploring perhaps variations on body shape, how the head and neck sit on a body, where the limbs are attached, whether the limbs are attached at the same point or at different points on the figure, whether the limbs are separate or cut as a pair and move as one piece, whether any of the joints need to have their movement limited, how to avoid certain parts catching together, modifications to controls or where they are attached to the figure. Such explorations often reveal possibilities that enhance a puppet's movements or characterization.

## PUPPET ORIENTATION

Shadow figures are frequently represented by convention partly in profile, partly straight on, which is readily acceptable on the shadow screen. The Javanese *wayang kulit* figures, for example, are designed with the head, legs and feet viewed side-on while the body is presented almost full-frontal. Some of these traditional figures show both eyes even though the face is in profile, a technique adopted by some contemporary shadow designers. This stylized

depiction of the figure is akin to the images in Egyptian and Greek art, such as pottery decoration, and is similar to the approach to design adopted by Lotte Reiniger, an immensely skilful designer and exponent of shadow theatre and silhouette film. She argued that the full profile often limits the possibilities for characterization, producing figures that appear far too stiff. She would create the head in profile but turn the body partly forwards to show each shoulder, bringing both arms and both legs into view and increasing considerably the decorative possibilities, the scope for expression and the visual impact of the figures.

Consider the entire head and body shape, including the cut of the hair. The angle of the head, for example, can suggest confidence, haughtiness, modesty, submissiveness or sadness. The angle of the neck and back, the position

of the hands and feet, all contribute to characterization. Study people of different ages, sizes and shapes, at rest, moving, at work, at play, and in different moods.

## DECORATION AND COLOUR

Do your figures require decoration? Study the Javanese shadow puppets whose strong but balanced contrast between surface and cutaway decoration contributes to their visual impact. Indian and Chinese shadow puppets use such methods too. Sometimes Chinese faces are extensively cut away so that only a fine outline of the profile and essential features remain (*see* pages 16 and 23).

You can enhance your design by cutting or punching shapes in the puppet or by covering cutaway sections with

LEFT: *Three examples of how Lotte Reiniger presented her figures, partly in profile and partly turned in order to maximize the scope for characterization.*

### About-face?

Be clear about which way each figure is to face when in use and remember that the audience will view the figures and scenery in the opposite way from the manipulators. Years of experience convinced Lotte Reiniger that an entrance from the left (the operator's right) 'makes the audience more receptive to the action of the performer. One might say that the movement from the left is the question, the movement from the right is the answer.'

ABOVE: *A strong but simple cut-out design to show a figure full-face.*

loosely woven materials that provide pattern or texture. How much it is possible to cut away depends on the material used, but take care not to weaken the figure or you will need some form of reinforcement. Try to avoid very narrow parts too for the same reason, alternatively, you might attach the textured materials to clear acetate shapes.

You may find it profitable to experiment with a range of materials that provide opportunities to achieve variety of movement as well as texture or decoration. Stretchy or flexible materials create interesting shapes and flowing fabrics can add a range of natural movements to a figure.

Colour may be added in traditional ways or with modern methods, and coloured, translucent materials can be used in conjunction with textured materials for a combined

**FIGURES USING TEXTURE AND COLOUR BY JANE PHILLIPS'S CARICATURE THEATRE, CARDIFF.**

*RIGHT: Textured materials attached to clear acetate provide detail in this figure from* Rhitta the Bearded, *a shadow play within a play (of* Blodeuwedd *or* The Flower Maiden*) designed by Geoffrey Evans.*

*BELOW LEFT: A single block of colour is used together with solid black areas for Sali Mali, a character from books of the same name by Mary Vaughan Jones, used to teach Welsh to young children; the arms are operated by a downward pull of a string, like a jumping jack.*

*BELOW RIGHT: Full colour was used for* The Emperor's New Clothes, *a Caricature production designed by Frank Koller for BBC TV Wales.*

effect. Colour can enhance a performance and help to create beautiful pictures, but I also find it refreshing to return to crisp, black and white images, sometimes with just a hint of colour.

*These boldly modelled figures were used both as rod puppets and as shadow figures in* Starchild, *a rock musical with puppets by Barry Smith's Theatre of Puppets.*

## THREE-DIMENSIONAL FIGURES

Three-dimensional objects and figures permit the exploration of the 'puppets' as seen from various angles. Solid objects with Perspex or acetate parts have interesting properties and shadow play using three-dimensional, wire puppets has possibilities too. Three-dimensional puppets that are boldly designed have on occasions been used both in front of and behind a shadow screen to good effect.

## APPROACHES TO DESIGN

Approaches to design are many and varied. You might draw first in detail and then cut out the figure, draw only a rough outline and then cut, adding detail as you go, or cut directly without any drawing, like some silhouette artists. Some figures by Jonathan Hayter (Figure of Speech puppet company) started out as a spontaneous cutting process, 'drawing with scissors', and these designs formed the

EXAMPLES OF JONATHAN HAYTER'S SPONTANEOUS CUTTING PROCESS.
BELOW: *Explorations with the relative positions of images 'drawn with scissors' form the basis for further puppet imagery.*
BELOW MIDDLE AND RIGHT: *Spontaneous cut-out shapes were used to determine the final design for The Philosopher, which was created with a collage of coloured tissue paper, cellophane and acrylic paint on a PVC base, for* Shadowplay, *a combination of animated film and live performance.*

*FAR LEFT: Mr Punch as a shadow, designed by the late Lotte Reiniger for the author.*
*LEFT: Mr Punch: the actual figure cut in card; the scribbled outline, still visible, is the way Reiniger established the basic shape; she added the detail as she cut the figure with scissors.*

*BELOW: The Lion, by Richard Bradshaw, is cut in thin, flexible, marine ply; it swallows the bee which subsequently emerges under its tail; it does not walk so there is a rod to each front foot, to the head, the body and the tail; a trigger on the head rod moves the eyelid, the jaw is joined to the body and the head is joined to the jaw at a different point so that the movement of the head rod can cause both the head and the jaw to move.*

basis for the final figures that were created with a variety of media.

Lotte Reiniger would quickly draw a rough shape for its general proportions and would then set to work with her scissors, chatting away as she created the fine detail of the figure. But she had an amazing ability and was able to analyse and visualize the components of each movement of each figure, which she achieved through years of careful observation – of people at rest, at work, at play, sitting, standing, walking, running, moving happily, sadly, and so on.

When designing a figure it is therefore a good idea to study the kinds of movement that would be characteristic of the person, to make sketches of the character in different poses or performing different actions. Consider proportion, and particularly the outline of the figure, including the outline of the costume and any designs or motifs upon it, which can convey a good deal of information. It is particularly helpful to study caricatures as the artist will have identified and exaggerated the salient characteristics or profiles of the individual depicted.

## DESIGNING ANIMAL FIGURES

Makers of three-dimensional puppets often say that they have more difficulty in making convincing animals than human figures, but they do not say the same of shadows. Animals have such diverse shapes that they offer many possibilities for shadow play, which also lends itself well to fantastic creatures such as dragons and other magical or mythical creatures.

When designing animals you can cut head, neck and body as a single unit with no joints or you can articulate the head. For this, either design the head and neck in one piece and make a joint between the neck and the body, or make the neck separately, with joints to both the head and the body.

*The unicorn has the head and neck as separate parts and just two controls; it was made by Paul Doran from X-ray film slightly coloured with ink; joints are nylon thread with the ends melted to form a tiny bobble.*

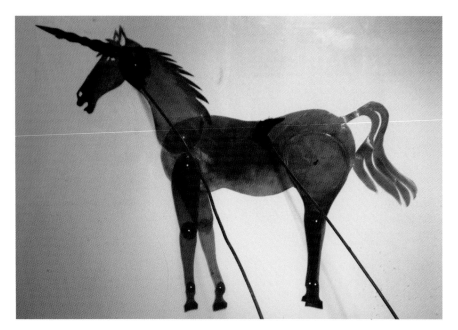

THREE OF SHADOWSTRING'S ANIMAL FIGURES IN WHITE CARD, COLOURED AND OILED.
*ABOVE: The elephant, by Jessica Souhami, has no neck; the head joins directly to the body with controls to the top of the head, the trunk and the body (see also page 87).*
*ABOVE RIGHT: These underwater animals are jointed to give sufficient flexibility without sagging in the middle as they move; children's workshop puppets from* No Trees No Life.
*RIGHT: The frog, from* No Trees No Life, *is depicted in profile and has only the single leg, which is adequate for the actions it performs.*

Plan for as many joints as are required within the body, but take care not to construct too many unsupported body sections that will simply sag when held up to the screen. It is common, particularly with animals, not to show all the limbs or to have one fixed and one articulated limb.

As with human figures, careful observation of animals will enhance your perception and your designs. Lotte Reiniger told entertaining stories of the many hours she sat in the zoo, not just observing the animals but mimicking some of their movements until she really had grasped not only their main features of body shape but also the essential components of their movements, whether slow and deliberate, ponderous and lumbering, stealthy, running, bounding, leaping or swinging.

## Information Resources for Drawing

There is no substitute for first-hand observation, but there are many resources available today, including the internet, that will complement observation and help you to focus your observations. Of particular use are good 'how to draw' books that will assist you in identifying the key elements of human and animal structure and show how to achieve convincing figures. Those books that build up the figures step by step from basic geometric lines and shapes are among those that I have found to be most useful, whether produced for children or adults.

For animals, natural history museums are wonderful resources. Remember that your designs do not have to be naturalistic and you can modify shape, scale and proportion for visual and dramatic effects. In this respect, books on how to draw cartoon characters help in understanding the essence of a creature and aspects of caricature involved in these will inform the process of simplification and selection in shadow puppet design.

## Controls

Shadow puppets are normally controlled from below or behind by means of stiff wires or rods. Occasionally, they are suspended like a marionette on strings but, with some notable exceptions, this is generally more problematic to operate and stage successfully. Most figures have one main supporting rod that effects the general movement of the figure. While a great deal of movement can be achieved with this single control, many productions will require more sophisticated gestures that call for additional control, most

*This figure, made in thin plywood, has three control rods, one to the upper body, one to the hand and another to one foot; made by Steve and Chris Clarke, for Shadowstring Theatre.*

frequently for the arms but also for legs, head or mouth – but not all at once.

Try to keep the 'mechanics' of the figure as simple as possible, particularly in relation to the extent of the controls. Generally, the simpler the control the better it will work, and the more complicated the controls the more difficult they will be to manipulate, so restrict controls to the minimum necessary to achieve the desired effect, and certainly not more than you can hold and manipulate. Make the most of the puppet's natural movement and let this play on the imaginations of your audience. They will read much into the merest hint of movement.

If you have a complex problem, first try to find a simple solution or to simplify the problem. It is better to modify a detail in the performance or an action that the puppet is required to perform rather than create an over-complex solution that might prove cumbersome in performance.

## GROUPED FIGURES

Groups of figures that are to act in unison may be created as a single cut-out unit and will often require some kind of support, such as a thin wooden batten, strip of card or piece of strong acetate or wire if you wish to keep them in one plane during use. They may be attached to some form of common control with a simple mechanism to achieve simultaneous movement.

Alternatively, they may be attached to a common control while permitting parts of the individual figures to move naturally with no direct form of control, though the momentum of the group will have an influence on these movements. When planning such groups, remember that crowd or battle scenes do not have to be represented by sets of figures lined up behind each other. They can be stacked vertically or linked in different patterns within the screen.

*Soldiers going into battle, viewed from both sides of the screen at Shadowstring Theatre; they are cut from black X-ray film and attached to a single base strip.*

# 4  SHADOW PUPPET CONSTRUCTION

Shadow puppets can be as simple or as complex as required, starting from a basic cut-out shape with no moving joints. However, you will find that they are greatly enhanced by some movement, which may be achieved just by adding fabrics or trimmings that move with the momentum of the figure. Fully articulated puppets offer much wider possibilities and require little more in terms of controls. Indeed, one basic control rod used for a simple cut-out figure can achieve a considerable range of movements with a jointed figure. This chapter describes the methods for constructing shadow figures in a variety of materials. Subsequent chapters describe how to add detail, decoration and colour and how to control and manipulate the figures. As you move from design to construction you will find it helpful to have a simple screen or a light box at hand so that you can check the figure as you make it.

## TOOLS

At the very simplest level you can make fully articulated shadow puppets with no more than a pencil, a pair of scissors and a hole punch, but a good set of tools would include:

- pencils and erasers
- felt pens
- craft knives (fine and large) and scalpel
- scissors (various)
- needles (sewing and darning)
- pliers, side cutters (for wire)
- punches: paper, single-hole, leather
- awl
- stapler, staple gun, staples
- small hammer (e.g., tack hammer)

*OPPOSITE PAGE:*
*One-Man-Band from* Three Animal Acts *by Christopher Leith's Shadow Show; the figure is made from parchment paper, coloured with translucent inks.*

*THIS PAGE:*
*A selection of useful tools: scissors, scalpel, craft knife, staplers and metal rule.*

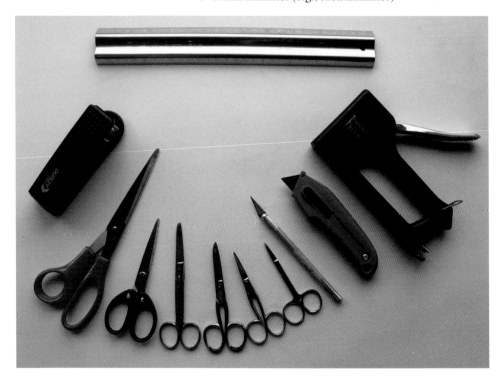

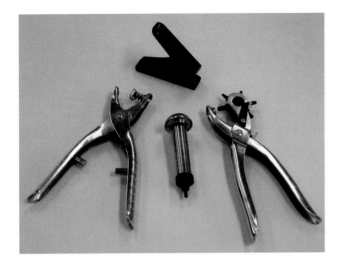

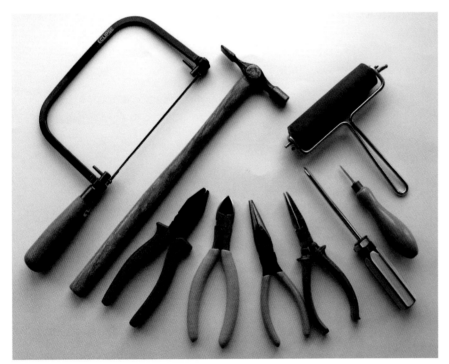

*ABOVE LEFT:* *A variety of hole punches.*
*ABOVE:* *Eyelet tool and eyelets.*
*LEFT:* *Coping saw, tack hammer, selection of pliers, side cutters, screwdriver, awl and roller.*

- roller
- coping saw, fretsaw
- eyelet punch and eyelets
- adhesives (depending on the materials used): UHU clear adhesive and PVA are always useful
- cellotape, masking tape, duck tape
- threads (nylon, braided nylon), cord, string
- screwdriver and screws
- rivet-type paper fasteners, paper binders.

## MATERIALS

Traditionally, shadow puppets have been made from a fairly rigid, robust, sheet material. In the east, hide treated to make it translucent and coloured with dyes has long been favoured, sometimes also gilded. In the west, cardboard and three-ply wood are more common, but today figures are also cut from a range of materials such as lampshade parchment, parchment paper, acetate, X-ray film, fabrics,

ABOVE: *A witch designed by Jessica Souhami for Shadowstring Theatre; it is cut from black card and jointed with nylon thread.*
RIGHT: *The soldier was cut from thin plywood for Shadowstring Theatre by Steve and Chris Clarke.*

flexible mirrors or sheet metal, including aluminium, tin or zinc. Take care with the thickness of any material you choose, if it is too thick, it might be difficult to cut but if it is too thin relative to its height, it might become floppy and unmanageable.

If you require the shadow to have a sharp outline, keep this in mind when selecting the material and choose one that will give a clean edge when it is cut. If you want a figure that can change its shape, then a plastic or fabric will better suit your purpose. Figures that will be subject to a good deal of wear and tear are obviously best made from a fairly strong material.

## Cardboard

For mainly black images, fairly stiff, smooth card is suitable for shadow puppets up to approximately 50cm (20in) high. Black card is not essential but is preferable because some thin screen materials will allow unwanted colour or printing on the card to show through. Cereal box cardboard is a cheap alternative and has about the right thickness; if the inside is plain, face this towards the screen and you will achieve a good shadow but if there is printing on the inside of the box, paint it black to ensure that the markings cannot show through the screen. You might paint it black anyway to increase the intensity of the shadow. To strengthen the card coat it with PVA medium on both sides. Mounting card that is black on one side and white on the other is useful as it provides a light surface for drawing the shape and a black surface to face the screen.

## Plywood

Plywood is ideal for figures over 50cm (20in) high. Three-ply is suitable, but thicker ply may create blurred shadows with some types of lighting if the figure has moving parts because these will be too far from the screen to give a sharp outline.

LEFT: *The Turkish Karagöz, cut from hide; the hat is pivoted on the head and has an additional strip of hide to limit the degree of movement.*

*Jack with the Giant from* Jack and the Beanstalk *by Christopher Leith's Shadow Show; parchment paper coloured with translucent inks.*

Cut the outline and internal decoration with a fretsaw or coping saw and, where appropriate, a drill. Sand the surfaces and edges thoroughly so that they are perfectly smooth before making the joints (*see* pages 62–63).

## Hide

Traditional Chinese figures are created from hide from the belly of a donkey as it is the thinnest part of the skin. Indonesian puppets use deer or buffalo hide; in Thailand deerskin is preferred, stained with red and green dyes. If you intend to make your shadow figures by these traditional methods you will find that the best sources are suppliers of parchment for book-binding and drums and other percussion instruments.

The tools you will need depend on the extent and nature of the planned detail and the decoration and thickness of the parchment. A craft knife and scalpel may be sufficient for some purposes while more elaborate work might require a set of carving tools. An Indonesian shadow puppet maker might use up to thirty different chisels in a variety of sizes and cutting edges to obtain the fine filigree effects of the *wayang kulit* puppets.

## Parchment Paper and Lampshade Parchment

Certain types of parchment are excellent materials for full-colour figures as they are already translucent and so need no additional treatment after being coloured with translucent inks. Parchment is a good alternative to hide as it is much easier to cut and produces a similar effect when coloured.

Some makers have used lampshade parchment, but Christopher Leith has produced wonderful coloured figures by using different thicknesses of parchment paper, a heavier weight for the head and body and a slightly lighter one for the limbs. Alternatively, provided that it is translucent, you can use a lightweight parchment card.

## Black Styrene or Plasticard

Styrene is a high-impact polystyrene which is sold under a variety of trade names such as Plasticard. It is a type of plastic used in modelling and it can be cut, filed, drilled and shaped. Cut it with a sharp scalpel or craft knife, but rather than cutting right through it, you can cut partly through and then snap off the waste, although this is easier with straight-line cuts. The edge might need scraping and sanding to clean it up. For an adhesive use polystyrene cement or the solvents available in model shops; the solvent effectively 'welds' the plastic together.

## Other Plastics and Film

Old, unwanted plastic document folders are a useful source of material for figures of modest size provided that they are not too flimsy to remain upright when in use. They are easily cut with scissors or a craft knife and it is possible to achieve a very crisp outline. Black is probably best for opaque, black figures as some colours may be slightly translucent, depending on their thickness, although this is sometimes a desirable feature.

A good alternative is used X-ray film, which has sufficient firmness coupled with a degree of flexibility. It is also strong and durable. Clear plastic sheets, comparable to strong cardboard, make a good base for some types of full-colour figure. Jonathan Hayter (Figure of Speech company)

*Backstage and audience views of a dragon cut from X-ray film with circular joints; controls are attached to head, tail and the centre of the body with Velcro, Shadowstring Theatre.*

uses vac-forming plastic sheets, which have proved highly suitable for shadow figures. They are not put through the vac-forming process but used simply in their original state.

## Perspex

Perspex (acrylic glass or Plexiglass) is useful for a number of applications. You can draw the figures on this transparent base, make full-colour figures or create figures that have a mixture of black and coloured (and/or clear) parts. It comes in varying thicknesses: 2–3mm (about 0.1in) is suitable. A translucent form of Plasticard (sheet styrene in the USA), described on page 51, is similar to the material used for CD jewel cases.

Draw the outline with a fine, water-based felt pen and cut out the parts with a fine saw blade such as a fretsaw. Add the detail with black paint and/or transparent, glass-painting colours. To avoid brush strokes, use an airbrush or spray paints, but take care not to overspray parts already painted. Reinforce vulnerable parts by gluing on another layer of Perspex with an adhesive manufactured for the purpose. Some will give immediate adhesion but others may need an ultraviolet lamp to harden them quickly; sunlight will be much slower. Joints are described on pages 60–63.

## Acetate

Acetate, such as that used with an overhead projector, is useful if it is sufficiently thick. Very flimsy acetates may be too floppy when held up to the screen, or too brittle and insufficiently sturdy for the rigours of shadow play and likely to tear at the joints.

Images can be created in the same ways as described above for Perspex figures. Layers of acetate can be used for

*Parvati from* **Rama,** *constructed by Jonathan Hayter with acrylic paint on PVC.*

*FAR LEFT: Caricature Theatre's Welsh dragon, painted on acetate, from the legend of how it came into being with the conflict between the red and the white dragon.*
*LEFT:* The Cat Came Back *by Richard Bradshaw; the balloon and basket are made from four overlapping pieces of clear plastic so that they can 'explode'.*

*A metal figure and the shadow it creates; note the power of the shadow compared with that of the actual figure.*

added strength or to sandwich materials between the layers. Join them with staples or sew them together with strong, fine thread. To prevent the staples or stitching from showing, position them carefully so that they are hidden by the design.

The use of clear glue is possible but is not always satisfactory as it can sometimes appear as a visible blob or even discolour over time and become increasingly obtrusive. Some glues will eat into or warp an acetate sheet, so always test possible ones on a sample before working on the actual figure. Acetate is also used to strengthen figures made from other materials.

## Sheet Metal

Cut and shape sheet aluminium, zinc or tin with tinsnips or a hacksaw with thin blades; finish off with files. Be aware that it is not so easy to achieve fine detail with these materials. However, Roscolab Ltd, who supply the gobos shown in the chapter on lighting and sound (*see* page 156), will cut figures to your design from a metal gobo. They will provide you with the figure and the disc from which it is cut so that you have a positive and a negative

image, suitable for projection. The small metal figure shown on page 9 was created in this way.

## Flexible Materials

Flexible materials, such as fabrics, create interesting, flowing shapes. You can attach the fabric directly to control rods or wires, but it is used more frequently with other materials (*see* pages 54, 68 and 71). Construct key parts in a solid material to ensure the secure attachment of controls and to give form or emphasis to the figure. Sheet rubber or tubing can be used for parts of a figure and it can be as flexible or as stiff as required. String and nets are useful for suggesting hair.

## Natural Materials

You might use natural materials such as grasses, reeds and pressed leaves to achieve a variety of shapes and textures that are particularly useful for scenery, either projected or held against a shadow screen. They may be held within projector slides, sandwiched between sheets of acetate or used unprotected to benefit from natural movement, in which case they are likely to need frequent

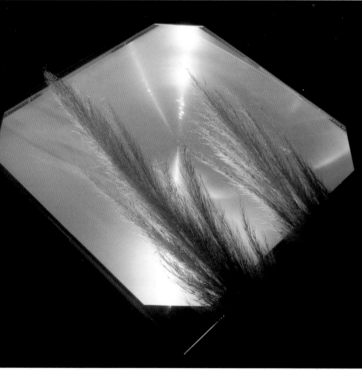

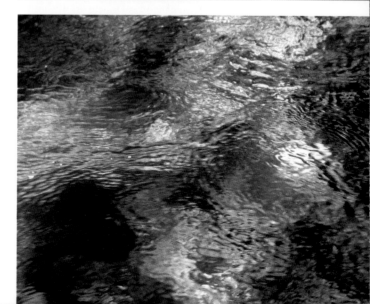

TOP: *Flexible materials used with large projections and small figures in Gilgamesh by Teatro Gioco Vita, Italy.*
ABOVE: *Grasses used for scenic projections.*
RIGHT: *Photographic images of water were photocopied on to acetate for projection across an entire screen.*

replacement. Photographs of suitable natural images might also be copied on to acetate and used for texture or for scenery.

## BASIC SHADOW PUPPETS

At the most basic level, you can draw your design directly on to cardboard simply as a silhouette outline. Cut out the shape with sharp scissors and add one of the controls described in the chapter on shadow puppet control (page 83).

However, it is always a good idea to design your figures on paper first and with due regard for their relative sizes and the dimensions of the screen. Next, transfer each design on to a sheet of cardboard. You can do this by cutting out your paper design and using this as a template or by using carbon paper. If you are using card that is black on one side and white on the other, ensure that you copy the image on to the white side the correct way round: your view will be the reverse of that seen by the audience. If the card is entirely black, you might use white carbon paper (available from art equipment suppliers). When cutting out your figures, you might add detail, decoration or colour as described in the chapter on detail, decoration and transformation (page 67).

## STRENGTHENING THE FIGURE

If you find that there are any weak areas of the figure, glue on additional pieces of card to strengthen it and strengthen any narrow areas with galvanized wire, glued and taped on securely.

Alternatively, you might use a clear contact adhesive to affix a piece of strong acetate to the entire figure. Attach the acetate before trimming it to the shape of the card. Instead of cutting away the gaps that have caused the weakness, you could leave the acetate intact since it will not show significantly on the screen.

## ALTERNATIVE MATERIALS

Rather than use cardboard, you might transfer your design on to thin plywood, opaque plastic or even sheet metal, using a cutting method appropriate to the material.

## ARTICULATED SHADOW PUPPETS

There are many ways to create articulated figures and their joints. The first description below sets out the basic process for a straightforward, cardboard, jointed figure, although a variety of materials could be used instead of

*This basic female figure, cut in black card, needed reinforcement with clear acetate glued on securely.*

## THE BASIC DESIGN PROCESS

*LEFT: The design for a wolf, showing the overlapping parts.*

*BELOW LEFT: The design is redrawn with all the overlapping parts separated.*

*BELOW RIGHT: The design is transferred to card and cut out.*

*BOTTOM: The wolf, assembled, appears as a shadow.*

card. The following sections detail a variety of methods for making the actual joints with different materials. In all instances they should be strong and move freely and smoothly.

**The Basic Process**
First draw your figure in silhouette on a sheet of paper. Mark the joints clearly, draw the overlapping parts and identify the point where they are to pivot. Remember that sometimes figures are made with a variety of joints, not just where they occur in humans. In your design round off moving parts as appropriate so that no sharp corners or unsightly curves stick out beyond the outline of the figure as it moves.

Copy the design to another sheet of paper with all the parts drawn separately without overlapping. To do this you might use carbon paper or simply trace over the initial design, for which a light box is helpful.

Transfer the design to card either by cutting out paper templates or by using carbon paper, as described above for basic shadow puppets. Mark clearly the position of the joints. Cut out the separate parts of the figure and make

clean holes at the pivotal points of overlapping parts. Double check that the outline of the figure is not compromised as the individual parts move; trim the edges further if necessary. At this point you might add any materials or coatings that may be required for strengthening purposes.

Join the parts together using one of the methods described below. Take care to arrange the separate parts in a stepped or scaled fashion, one on top of another, so that they will not catch together during use. Take account of which way the figure is to face on the screen; moving parts that are to have a control attached need to be on the operator's side of the figure or the movement of the control

*The Gorilla, an articulated figure by Richard Bradshaw; first a coconut falls on his head, then the palm fronds, with the tree following him as he tries to keep clear.*

*Combined separate parts of a figure are arranged in a scaled or stepped manner to prevent snagging.*

57

will be restricted by the body. When the joints are complete, the figure is ready for its controls to be attached, as described in the chapter on puppet control (*see* page 83).

### Making the Holes for Joints

Depending on the material used and the jointing method, you might use a needle, a paper punch, a leather punch, an awl or a drill to make a hole. A stationery punch may make holes too close to the edge of a figure and so a single-hole punch is a far superior tool and the many varieties of them allow you to adjust the size of the hole. Never use the point of your scissors to make a hole as they will not give a clean hole and you will soon spoil them for cutting the figures.

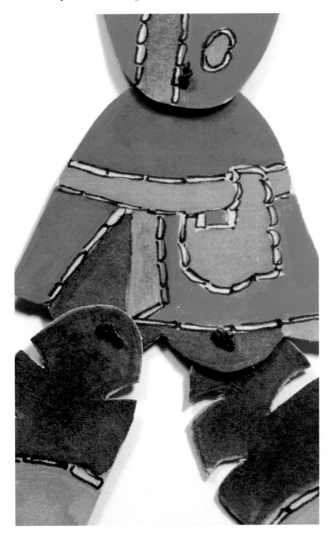

*Knotted thread joints.*

### Joints for Lighter Puppets

If the puppet is to be held flat against the screen, try to avoid joints with protrusions that would create an unsightly bump on the screen. Also avoid anything that might snag on the screen or arrange for the part that poses such a risk to be on the manipulator's side of the puppet. There is a number of quick and easy ways to construct these joints when the figures are not too heavy.

*Knotted thread or cord* facilitates joints that move freely and smoothly. It is advisable to rub the thread with beeswax before use to prevent fraying. I prefer Dacron braided nylon fishing line which is strong even without being waxed, but I always wax it as well just to be safe (although I confess I do not know whether this makes any difference). Thread the cord through a suitable needle and push it through the centre point of the overlapping parts. Knot the cord on each side of the joint; the knot on the first side is easy but getting the knot close enough on the other side is a little more tricky as you need it to be sufficiently tight to hold the joint as intended but not too tight or it will hinder smooth movement. Make the knot as close as possible to the joint, keeping the loop loose; hold the thread in one hand and, with your other thumb and forefinger, gently ease the loop down toward the joint as you increase the tension of the thread. If it looks like being too far from the joint, do not pull

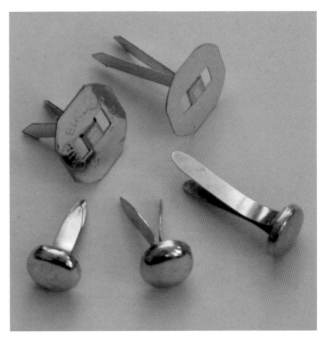

*Paper fasteners for joints.*

the thread tight but loosen it again and try to ease it down further. You can improve upon this by making subsequent knots between the first knot and the card. Seal the knots with a clear contact glue.

*Paper fasteners or binders* that are rather like split pins are useful for freely moving joints that are quick to construct, provided that you make clean holes first. They have a head and twin prongs that spread apart and can be pressed back flat to secure the parts to be joined.

Two types of paper fastener are commonly used. The brass fasteners tend to have rounded heads so try to use those that are not too bulbous. The other type has a flat head, it consists of a thin metal disc and a separate single strip that is folded in half to create two prongs. The prongs

fit through two slots in the metal disc, which fits very neatly against the puppet. Both types come in several sizes, so choose one with prongs of suitable length for the size of the puppets you are using. Very short prongs may not provide a sufficiently secure joint; very long ones may protrude beyond the edges of the puppet, unless the ends are cut off or folded back towards the centre and pressed well down.

Use a punch to make clean holes at the centre point of the overlapping parts. It is preferable to use a punch that makes small holes rather than a standard paper punch so that you do not need to use large-headed fasteners since the head must be sufficiently large as not to pass through the holes. Assemble the parts and insert the paper fastener

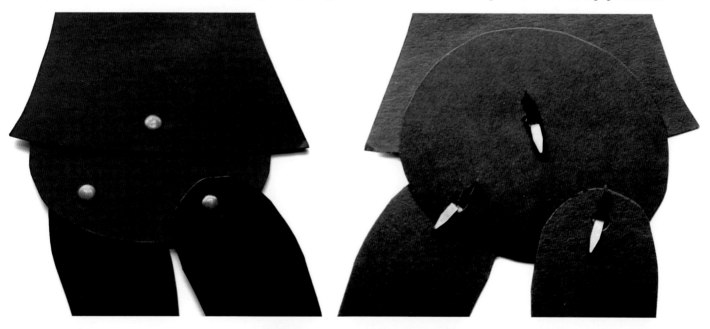

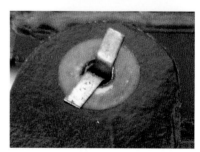

*ABOVE: Cardboard body sections joined with paper fasteners; the prongs must be pressed in to avoid snagging without restricting the movement of the joints.*
*RIGHT: The long ends of this fastener have been folded inwards and pressed down to avoid snagging.*
*FAR RIGHT: The ends of a long paper fastener were cut off to prevent their protruding beyond the figure.*

with the head on the side that is to face the screen. Separate the two prongs of the fastener and fold them back in opposite directions. Press them down as flat as possible without restricting movement.

*Fine wire* (for example, 15A fuse wire) coiled or twisted into a figure of eight shape on each side of the joint may be used for quite small figures. Alternatively, twist it into a figure of eight on one side of the joint and spread the ends out on the other side. Ensure that the screen side of the puppet has the wire in a figure of 8 because loose ends might snag the screen.

*Knotted nylon thread* (clear 4lb fishing line or strimmer nylon) is used for lightweight translucent puppets, such as those made from sheets of acetate. Follow the same procedure as described above for thread and cord. Seal the nylon knots with a spot of clear glue or carefully melt it into a bobble with a lighted taper or the tip of a soldering iron. If you place a small acetate washer on each side of the joint, glue or melt the knots on to the washers. Some makers simply melt the end of the nylon thread to the washer without making a knot; just a quick touch with a soldering iron is all that is required.

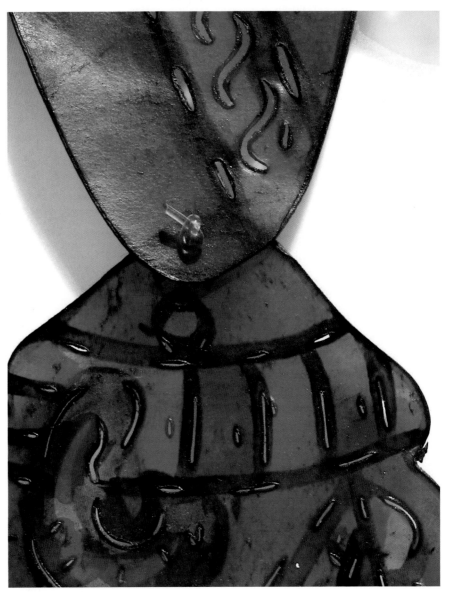

ABOVE: *Fine looped wire may be used to join acetate parts.*
RIGHT: *Strong nylon thread is suitable for joining translucent puppet parts, in this case hide.*

RIGHT: *A small bead has been used with nylon thread to make this joint in a clear PVC figure, by Nick Tasker (The Primary Puppets) for Shadowstring Theatre.*
BELOW: *An experimental joint by Paul Doran; the press stud was heated and pressed into the plastic sheet, 'welding' them together, a small hole punched in the limb snapped into place on the press stud.*
BELOW RIGHT: *X-ray film, tinted with ink, is joined using nylon thread with the ends melted to a tiny bobble with a lighted taper, a match or a soldering iron.*

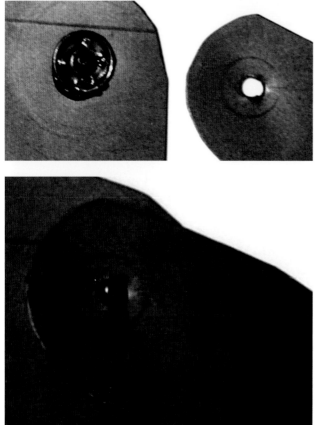

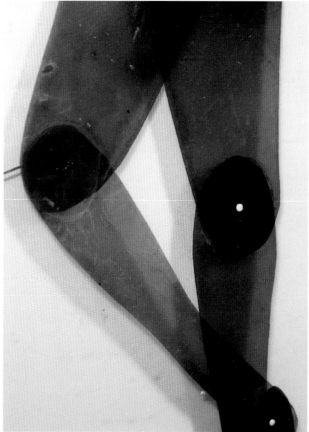

*OPPOSITE PAGE:*
JOINTS FOR PLYWOOD PUPPETS.
TOP LEFT: *Knotted thread on the side of the figure facing the operator.*
TOP RIGHT: *The reverse side (screen side) of the knotted thread joint; the cord is splayed and glued flat against the leg to avoid bumps pressing into the screen.*
BOTTOM LEFT: *A joint with galvanized wire looped and bent flat against the leg.*
MIDDLE RIGHT: *A screw joint.*
BOTTOM RIGHT: *A small nut and bolt joint.*

*THIS PAGE:*
JOINTS FOR WIRE FIGURES.
BELOW: *Interlocked, looped wires are able to move freely in any plane.*
BOTTOM: *Looped wires joined with small washers, nuts and bolts are designed to move in the same plane.*

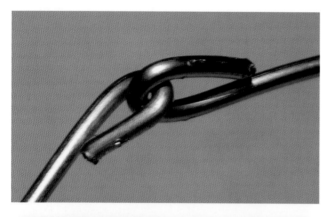

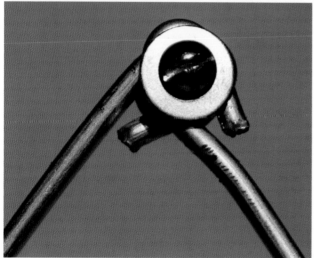

## Joints for Heavier Puppets

The joints used for heavier figures depend on the materials from which they are constructed.

*Knotted string* is suitable for plywood. At the pivotal point of the joint drill a small hole through each part to be joined. Knot one end of the string and thread the other end through the holes. How you secure the string on the other side of the joint depends on how the figure is to be used. If it is to be held clear of the screen with a projection style of lighting you can simply knot the second side too.

If the figure is to be held against the screen, a large knot on the screen side would be problematic. Instead, splay the ends of the string and glue them securely and as flat as possible to the plywood. This should be sufficiently strong to hold firm, but you might secure it further with a staple gun. Always check that the joints are secure before each performance.

*Galvanized wire* is sufficiently strong for joining plywood parts. Insert the wire through small holes drilled in the plywood and bend it into a loop on each side of the joint. Flatten the loops against the figure, ensuring that they do not impede movement.

*Screws* may also be used for plywood. The screw needs to be very secure in one part of the joint while the section adjacent to the screw head must have a sufficiently large hole for it to swing freely without loosening the screw. Use screws with countersunk heads and countersink any holes to accommodate them. Thin metal washers inserted between the moving sections help to facilitate smooth movement. Some shadow puppet makers working with Perspex would use a screw joint. They would drill one hole of a fractionally larger diameter than the screw and the other would be 0.5mm smaller than the screw. In the smaller hole a thread cutter is used to cut a thread of the exact size for the screw. The parts are assembled with the screw inserted through the larger hole, through a Plexiglas washer, and then screwed securely into the smaller hole.

*Small nuts and bolts* may be used with plywood, Perspex, sheet metal and other rigid materials. Carefully drill the holes for jointing and countersink the holes if the material permits this. Secure the joint with a small nut and bolt and use washers to assist free movement. Add a locking-nut to the bolt to ensure that it does not loosen during use.

## Joints for Wire Puppets

Wire puppets may be jointed by using interlocked loops in the wire, which will give loose, swinging movement. To restrict movement to one plane, place the loops together, not interlocked, and join them by using washers with small nuts and bolts, including a locking nut. Alternatively, insert a piece of wire through the joint and bend the ends flat against the washers.

## Washers

If everything works well without washers, do not use them just for the sake of it. Avoid anything that will prevent the puppet from being held closely against the screen. With lighter puppets, some makers cut three thin, acetate washers to place between, and outside, the moving parts to facilitate smooth movement, although many puppeteers find movement satisfactory without such washers. Heavier figures often benefit from the use of thin, metal washers, but these are not suitable for translucent puppets. Cut translucent washers from a piece of Perspex by using a hole-cutter attached to a drill. For the washer use the waste from cutting the hole.

## Restricted Joints

To restrict movement of any part or to prevent joints bending in the wrong direction, either link the moving parts with a piece of fine thread that is just long enough for the required movement or add additional strips of card or a piece of thin plywood at a suitable point on one of the jointed parts so as to act as a buffer for the other. The requirements of the action might call for some variation on these methods but the same basic principles will apply.

## Weighting the Figure

To aid movement, some performers glue a small piece of thin sheet lead or metal washers to the feet of their shadow puppets, on the operator's side. I have never found this to be necessary for puppets of a reasonable size that are to be used in live shows, as opposed to animated film where weighted parts are helpful. However, if the puppets are quite small, a little extra weight might prove useful.

## CARE OF THE PUPPETS

When the shadow puppets are not in use, store them flat and away from heat, damp and, if coloured, direct sunlight. It is helpful to make cardboard sleeves for each figure, this not only keeps them flat but also prevents their snagging each other when packed or when being taken out for use, which is when most snagging is likely to occur. Oiled figures, described in the next chapter, should be stored in polythene bags to prevent their drying out.

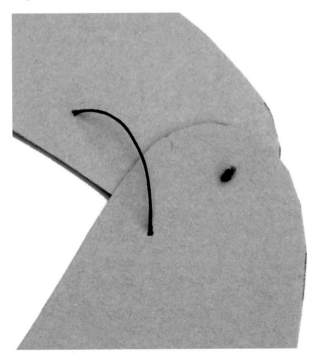 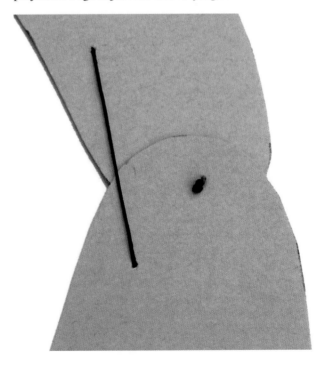

*Thread is used to restrict a joint from bending in the wrong direction.*

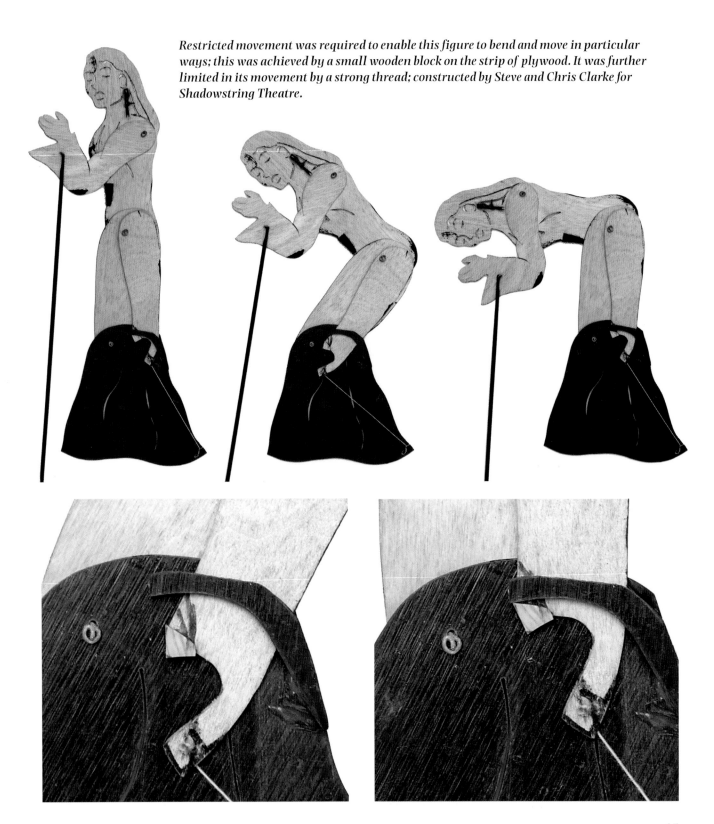

Restricted movement was required to enable this figure to bend and move in particular ways; this was achieved by a small wooden block on the strip of plywood. It was further limited in its movement by a strong thread; constructed by Steve and Chris Clarke for Shadowstring Theatre.

# 5 DETAIL, DECORATION AND TRANSFORMATION

## DETAIL AND DECORATION

You can elaborate the appearance of the basic silhouette by variations in pattern (cutaway design), tone (varying opacity), texture (partial or broken resistance to light) and colour.

### Pattern with Cutaway Design

Pattern is achieved by cutting out a design with a craft knife, a razor blade in a purpose-made holder or with a suitable hole punch. You can create the design with holes a little larger than pin-pricks, with filigree-type cuts made like the Javanese figures or with much bolder cuts.

Cut away parts of the silhouette to add detail to the face or hair, to show the line, folds or decoration of a costume, or to show the line of a limb if it is not articulated. This is also an excellent method to show animal markings. Sometimes Chinese faces are extensively cut away so that only a fine outline and essential features remain (*see* page 16).

If a design is cut in an articulated figure you may decide to avoid cutting away too close to the overlap of the joints both for strength and because the overlapping parts will obscure the pattern. If, for some reason, you need to cut towards the joint, glue a piece of clear acetate over any weak part. Rather than strengthening individual parts, you can apply adhesive to the entire puppet and press it on to a strong acetate sheet. Then cut out the acetate around the outline of the figure. *See also* page 76 for a description of the Chinese method for maintaining visible patterns with overlapping parts at the joints.

*OPPOSITE PAGE:*
*Ganesh made from painted and scratched acrylic for* **Rama** *by* **Figure of Speech.**

*THIS PAGE:*
*RIGHT: Cutaway lines give detail to the face and hair of this figure, made by Steve and Chris Clarke for Shadowstring Theatre.*
*BELOW: Cutaway sections of the dolphin emphasize its shape and add life to its movements.*

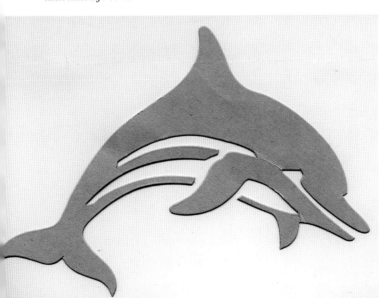

ABOVE: *Curtain net is used to give texture to a cutaway section of this figure's skirt.*

BELOW: *A wash of coloured lights over the screen, used with solid black figures and scenery cut from card and X-ray film;* Witch Is Which *by Shadowstring Theatre.*

## Tone

Variation in tone is achieved by using materials of differing opacity to cover the cutaway parts of the figure. Paper, tissue paper in multiple layers and semi-transparent fabrics such as chiffon or taffeta in layers or folds are some of the possibilities.

## Texture

Texture is created with fabrics that are loosely woven or any other material that has a partial or broken resistance to light. Examples include nets, mesh, scrim, wire netting or waste materials from which shapes have been punched out during manufacture. Cord, string, raffia, wool, feathers and objects found in the natural world are good for hair and other trimmings.

Such materials may be used to cover a small cutaway section of a figure or the entire figure may be cut as a frame rather than a solid piece with the hollow areas covered with textured materials. An outline shape of this type will need to be reinforced with acetate or cut from plywood or another, suitably strong material. Some textured materials may need to be sandwiched between sheets of acetate or stitched into two layers of clear polythene sheets. The polythene may be fixed in a card or plywood frame or used in a flexible manner.

## Colour

Colours can be introduced into shadow play in the figures, the scenery or as a wash of coloured lighting over all or part of the screen. Shadow play also incorporates colourful, translucent figures that produce images in full colour but,

with the exception of their colour, they are constructed and performed in the same way as other shadow puppets.

You can introduce a little colour into a black silhouette to good effect, such as with the wolf's eye which is illustrated here, or you can use colours with more extensive cut-out shapes outlined in black like a stained glass window. Colour can be achieved by the use of coloured, translucent materials such as lighting gels, acetate, cellophane, coloured tissue paper or greaseproof paper tinted with water colours. Lighting gels give stronger colour and are more durable.

Folding, pleating and crushing translucent or transparent materials, such as tissue paper or cellophane, can create a range of interesting shapes, tones and depths of colour.

*A little colour introduced into a solid black figure for the wolf's eye.*

*The effect of the wolf's coloured eye on the shadow screen.*

*Colour introduced into cut-out sections throughout the design by Jean Pierre Lescot, France.*

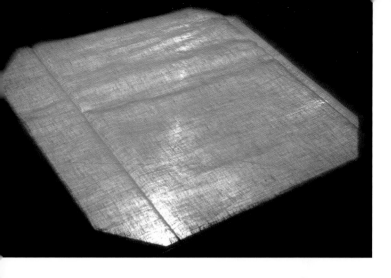

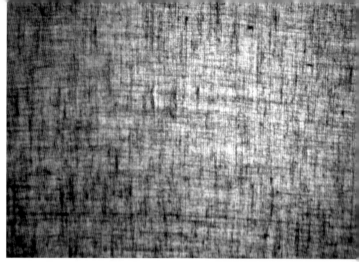

The effects produced by some materials might vary depending on whether the figure is held against the screen or projected from a distance. Some coloured materials will not produce the same quality of colour, if any, when projected, while others will work in both modes. Similarly, some fine, translucent, coloured fabrics may produce both colour and texture, but others may produce only texture, especially if the image is projected. Another possibility, but with limited application, is to play two different coloured lights on to the screen. Hold the figure in the light beam of one colour and the shadow appears in the other colour.

## IMAGES IN FULL COLOUR

You can achieve full colour with or without any black boundary lines by working on sheets of translucent acetate. The thickness of the acetate depends on the size of the figure, but it needs to be sufficiently thick to retain its shape. There are several possibilities for colouring the acetate:

- paint on the detail with glass painting colours or coloured, transparent varnish: an air brush or spray paint will give a more evenly painted finish and avoid brush strokes which may be more noticeable if the figure is projected larger on the screen;
- use layers of thin, coloured, transparent acetate;
- use coloured tissue paper or other coloured, translucent materials, attached with a transparent adhesive; or
- use self-adhesive coloured film such as Letrafilm.

LEFT: *A translucent figure of Mr Punch painted on clear PVC, by Nick Tasker for Shadowstring Theatre.*

ACRYLIC FIGURES BY CARICATURE THEATRE.
LEFT: *Punch and Judy figures for a shadow show have acrylic heads painted in translucent colours with black highlighting; fabric of various textures is used for the bodies.*
ABOVE AND BELOW: *The Monsters of Ignorance from* The Phantom Tollbooth *written by Norton Juster and directed by Jane Phillips.*

*Full-colour puppets created by Jessica Souhami by using traditional methods with modern materials.*

Overlaying coloured materials, rather than butting them together, creates a variety of colours and shades, but you need to experiment when overlapping colours as some will not give pleasing effects.

If necessary, highlight details or features in black paint or drawing ink with a fine brush on the reverse side of the acetate. Similarly, on the clear side you can introduce texture with other materials as described above. Covering the coloured materials with another layer of acetate will protect them from damage during use; this is also a useful way to stiffen a figure.

Plexiglas (acrylic glass) 2–3mm thick is a good, strong alternative to acetate as a base for coloured, transparent figures. Jonathan Hayter (Figure of Speech company) uses a variety of highly effective construction techniques to produce colourful images, including painted and scratched acrylic (*see* pages 32 and 66) and a combination of collage materials and acrylic varnish (*see* pages 41 and 82).

## FULL-COLOUR IMAGES IN THE TRADITIONAL STYLE

There is quite a simple, and highly effective, method for creating full-colour puppets in card along the lines of traditional oriental puppets. Plain card is coloured with felt pens or inks and treated with oil to make it translucent, as described below. The best card to use is matt Ivory Board,

the thickness of which is indicated by its weight per square metre; for figures up to 60cm high use 335g/sq.m card and for larger figures use 400g/sq.m. If you are using an alternative card, ensure that:

- it is thick enough to be rigid but not too thick or it will prove difficult to cut and to make it translucent;
- it has a matt surface or it will resist the colour and the oil;
- it is as white as possible so that it does not dull the colours; and
- it is not laminated since many laminated cards will not become translucent.

### Colours

For colouring, concentrated water colours are best, but felt tipped pens are satisfactory. Water-based pens are preferable to spirit-based ones as the colours of the latter tend to run when oiled. It is also better to use good quality pens with good points in a variety of styles. Thin pens are not good for filling in blocks of colour.

A range of water colours and transparent dyes is available, for example, Dylon, Luma Water Colours or, my preference, Dr Martin's Radiant Concentrated Water Colours. These really are concentrated so experiment in diluting them to different strengths and try mixing colours in different proportions and in different strengths

*Four figures based on* Arrow to the Sun: a Pueblo Indian Tale *by Gerald McDermott (Picture Puffin); the characters were based on this children's book as part of an activity combining shadow play with reading and other aspects of literacy in schools; the first image shows Ivory Board coloured with radiant watercolours with colour tests used before the colouring; the three other images show figures with different colouring styles: bold, brightly coloured and subtly coloured.*

of each. You will find a good range of possibilities emerging from such combinations and dilutions of the three colours Turquoise Blue, Daffodil Yellow and Tropic Pink. They come in small bottles with a dropper built into the cap so that you can measure out exactly the amount you require, a drop at a time. When you have determined a colour you wish to use for a figure, mix enough of it to complete the task rather than try to match it with a fresh mixture halfway through. Just in case you misjudge how much you need, always keep a careful note of the mixture and the dilution for each colour.

## Colouring

When you have designed the puppet, transfer the design lightly on to the white card; if it is articulated, remember to allow for the overlaps at the joints. Do not cut out the separate parts at this stage because there is a risk of damaging small cut-out parts when you come to the oiling stage. To produce a stronger colour, apply it to both sides of the card. To help you to do this accurately, when you have drawn the outline of the figure on to the card, turn it over and place it on a light box so that you can trace the design on the other side. In the absence of a light box, hold the card against a window, preferably in strong sunlight.

Colour the puppet with the chosen medium. If you colour only one side of the card, colour the one that will face the screen to help the colour to show more strongly. Take care to fill in each block of colour completely, light shading with white gaps is not effective for this technique. To achieve an even density of colour it helps with some media to dampen the card lightly with a brush before colouring. When using water colours or dyes, apply each colour separately to prevent their merging. Allow the figure to dry before proceeding to the next stage.

## Oiling

Lay the coloured sheet of card on a piece of paper towel on a protected work surface. Take another sheet of paper towel and fold or scrunch it into a wad for oiling the card. The best oil to use is liquid paraffin; cooking oil is a cheap but inferior alternative. Moisten the paper wad with the oil and coat the card with it, rubbing the oil in well. It is better to use too little at first and build up the oil gradually to give an even coating rather than risk flooding the card with oil.

If you look at the reverse side of the card at this point, you should see the oil coming through it, possibly with a somewhat blotchy effect and you will be able to see and attend to any parts that have not been oiled so evenly. Next

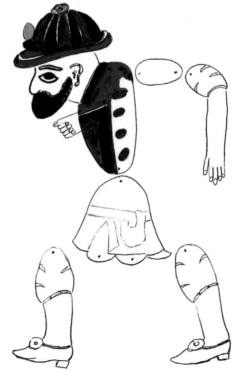

**CONSTRUCTING ARTICULATED FIGURES IN FULL COLOUR ON CARD.**
*FAR LEFT: The preliminary design for a version of Karagöz, showing the overlapping parts for joints.*
*LEFT: The design is transferred to white ivory board with the articulated parts separated and coloured before oiling, then cutting and assembling.*

*Figures in Ivory Board, coloured and oiled, by Jessica Souhami.*

**OVERLAPPING DESIGNS.**

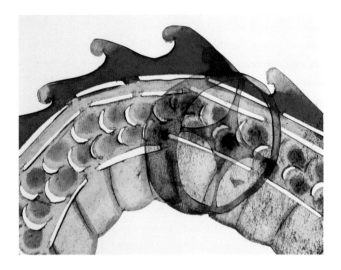 

*ABOVE*: *A four-spoke, cutaway section for the overlapping parts of an articulated, translucent Chinese dragon, to allow the design to show clearly.*
*ABOVE RIGHT*: *Similar cutaway sections for the leg tops of a Chinese figure.*

oil the other side of the card until all the colour shows through. The card is now translucent and stronger; hold it up to the light, areas not sufficiently oiled will be darker and any white areas somewhat grey. Use a clean sheet of paper towel to remove excess oil from the card and then cut around the outline of the shapes. If there are any potentially fragile areas, especially slender parts, it is best to leave white card between them and the rest of the figure; provided it is well oiled, the white area will scarcely show.

**Other Matters**

When making joints, it is helpful to place a small disc of clear acetate on each side of the joint to reduce wear of the card. Use knotted nylon thread or brass paper fasteners for the joints, as described in the chapter on puppet construction (page 47), but remember that paper fasteners will show on the screen so use the 'micro' or 'midget' variety and make suitably small holes to accommodate them. The overlapping parts tend to produce darker patches at the joints, obscuring any pattern. To overcome this, Chinese puppets are made with the design created in one part. The overlapping part has segments cut away to create what looks like a two-, three- or four-spoked wheel. This allows the main design to show through when the parts are joined.

For strengthening, coat the puppet with PVA medium: Rowney's PVA is waterproof and of good quality. Work on one colour at a time, applying the PVA carefully. Let each colour dry before starting on the next to prevent the colours from running. Repeat the process on the reverse side of the figure. This gives a hard plastic finish. There may be a tendency for overlapping parts to stick together and so, to avoid this, rub a little talcum power over the joints. An alternative is to glue clear acetate to the puppet, and this is useful also for repairs, but it is not easy to get it to adhere to the oiled surface. Most adhesives will not work and so it is essential not to have any surplus oil and to remove any surface oil carefully. Then some clear, contact adhesives like UHU should adhere.

Puppets that are simply oiled and not coated in any way should be stored in polythene bags to stop separate figures from sticking together and to prevent their drying out or they will need to be re-oiled carefully. I once stored a set of figures between the leaves of a large scrapbook and they dried out very quickly, losing a good deal of their translucence.

## FULL COLOUR WITH PARCHMENT

Select a suitable weight of translucent parchment paper, parchment card or lampshade parchment (*see* page 51). Transfer your design to the parchment lightly in pencil, allowing for joints as described previously. Colour the

*ABOVE: Jack and his Mother from Jack and the Beanstalk by Christopher Leith's Shadow Show; full colour figures on parchment paper, coloured with translucent inks.*

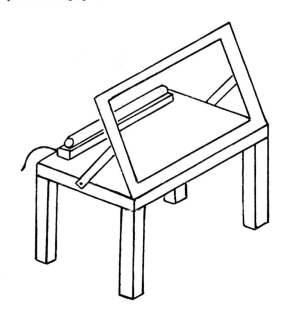

*An illuminated worktable for creating translucent figures.*

parchment with translucent inks. The coloured figure will be translucent without further treatment so you can cut it out, join any moving parts and add controls.

When colouring the parchment, you may find it helpful to place it on an opaque, illuminated surface that can be wiped clean of ink if necessary. A light box would serve the purpose, but Christopher Leith has designed a simple, angled surface that enables you to work in a more comfortable position. Place a sheet of smooth tissue paper between two sheets of glass that are held in a wooden frame, hinge the frame to a base board and secure the frame at the required angle with supporting struts. Place the parchment on the glass and illuminate the underside of the frame with a suitable domestic light. You can use the unit on a table top or attach separate legs to have it free-standing.

For joints, thread pushed through the card with a needle and knotted on either side of the joint is a suitable method to minimize their visibility. A variety of controls, described in the next chapter, is possible, but for his figures Leith used the type made from steel model wire with a fine loop on the end (*see* page 91). He attached these with strong thread to the edge of the figure, which had been reinforced with a small piece of acetate. This reduces the visibility of the controls and enables the figure to be turned around with a quick, smooth, flicking action.

## TRANSFORMATIONS

In shadow play your actors can transcend human limitations even more than three-dimensional puppets. They can assume any shape or size, transform into other characters or dissolve away before your eyes. In some ways they offer many of the possibilities available to cartoon film makers. Figures and scenes can be transformed and other effects achieved in a variety of ways. You may well invent some of your own but the principles are described in the following examples. (Transformations using multiple projections are described on pages 135 and 150.)

### Transformation by Substitution

Softer forms of lighting allow the image to fade as the figure is moved away from the screen. This enables you to substitute one figure for another, but practise the manoeuvre until it is smooth and convincing. You can achieve similar effects with two projectors, cross-fading to change one image into another.

If you need a shadow figure to have a variety of expressive hand gestures, cut out substitute hands and arms and mount them on a wire or strip of strong acetate and hold them in place. The original arm that is attached to the puppet needs to be positioned so that it will hang completely out of sight. This may also be a useful device for other applications in shadow play.

### Transformation by Revelation

Solid black figures make concealment or disguise possible so that a puppet or a piece of scenery can be unfolded, or a hidden part rotated into view, to transform a character or a setting.

To show a trail of liquid, use a piece of stiff cardboard scenery with a suitably shaped, cut-out section. Cover the cut out area with another piece of shaped card that slides

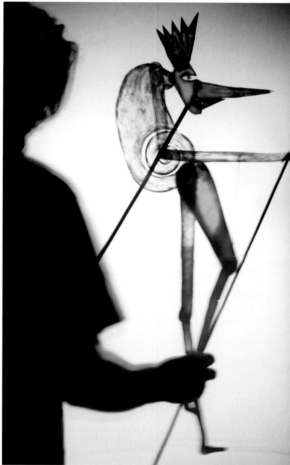

in grooves made from strips of card. At the appropriate moment, the sliding shape is moved, revealing the cut-out area beneath it and creating the appearance of running water or spilt milk. Some reveals can be even simpler, like the gingerbread man who emerges from a baked sheet. In this case the cut-out shape is placed back securely into the original card and, when removed, dances around leaving its negative image in the baked sheet.

## Transformation by Rotation

Scenery can be transformed using two interlocked, cut-out shapes that are rotated in the beam of a suitable strong light (such as a halogen lamp). Cut out the two separate shapes of equivalent height; at the points where they are to be joined cut in one scene a slot extending up from the base and in the other a slot extending down from the top. The slots should be just long enough for the base of each scene to be aligned.

Attach the structure to a rod. To do this, cut two slots at right angles to each other down through a dowel rod. Make the slots sufficiently long for the interlocked scenes to slide into them and be held securely. You might secure this with adhesive or omit the adhesive to enable the structure to be dismantled for packing, but, if you decide to do the latter, the execution of your cuts must be very precise to hold the scenes securely. The assembled unit is fixed on some small shelf or other device in front of the lamp. Place it square to the lamp so that only one scene is visible and there is no hint of the other. The transformation to the second scene is usually more effective if the unit is rotated slowly and steadily rather than hastily. The same method can be used to transform one character into another, but this is not as satisfactory as with scenery which may be secured to ensure that the shapes are turned just at the right moment. By contrast, it is difficult to maintain a moving character absolutely square between

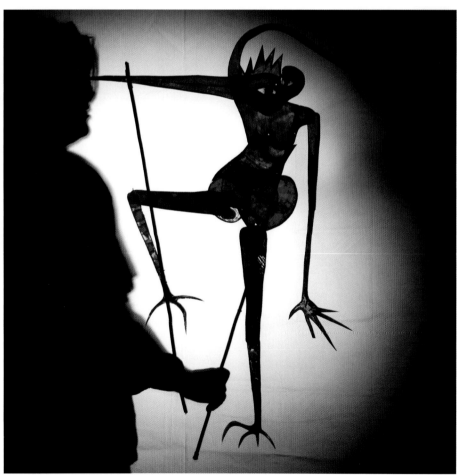

**TRANSFORMATION BY SUBSTITUTION:** *Moontime, a multi-media show by Figure of Speech; these transformations were developed after looking at alchemy as a source of the imagery of change and transformation.*

*OPPOSITE PAGE:*
TRANSFORMATION BY REVELATION:
*shadow puppets are ideal for hiding parts that are
subsequently revealed; this puppet was designed
originally in card by Jessica Souhami and recreated
in X-ray film by Paul Doran, Shadowstring Theatre.*

*THIS PAGE:*
TRANSFORMATION BY ROTATION:
*these figures, interlocked at right angles to each other, are
secured with one figure square to the screen. They are then
rotated steadily to reveal the new pose; figures created
by Anna Welbourne for the DaSilva Puppet Company's
production of Kipling's* The Cat That Walked by Himself.

light and screen and not give an untimely glimpse of part
of the second image.

## Transformation by Fire

Companies have sometimes set a figure alight to create a
transformation. The figure to be revealed is either created
in thin sheet metal or covered completely in aluminium
foil. To this shape is attached a paper version of the figure
that is to disappear; it should hide the other figure from
view. The paper is set alight and, as it burns, the ashes
float away to reveal the metal or aluminium-clad figure
beneath. Obviously you have to use a method of lighting
that allows the figure to be held well clear of the screen.

# 6 SHADOW PUPPET CONTROL

## PRINCIPLES OF CONTROL

Right from the initial design you will have determined whether your performance requires controls that are operated vertically, horizontally or at some other angle. I have a preference for hinged rods that can be held at any angle to the screen, but these will not necessarily be practical for every application.

Holding a control either horizontally or at an angle of up to 45 degrees to the figure is better if you need to keep it flat against the screen and makes it easier to use the whole screen on different levels. Horizontal operation requires the performers to stand behind the screen, which has implications for how and where you position the lighting and what forms of lighting can be used.

Figures operated horizontally or at an angle are not normally able to turn around, but a duplicate figure overcomes this limitation. Some traditional figures occasionally have the control rod attached to a hinge that is secured to the edge of the puppet's body. When it needs to be turned around, a quick flick of the control is all that is required, but it takes some skill to handle a puppet when its control is placed at an edge rather than at the natural point of balance.

Vertical operation, by comparison, keeps open the possibility of most types of lighting, except from below the screen, and facilitates the use of projected images. It enables figures to turn around but it is not so easy to keep them flat against the screen and it is essential that there is nothing on the staging or sets to restrict this.

Hinged controls, on the other hand, offer the benefits of both of these methods and reduce their limitations. They enable you to keep the figures against the screen fairly easily while working from a slightly, or significantly, lower position clear of any light beam. This facilitates a wide range of possibilities for both action and lighting. With most forms

*OPPOSITE PAGE:*
*Astral Angel, created by Jonathan Hayter for* Moontime, *can be used as a shadow or as a projection surface for multi-media video productions.*

*THIS PAGE:*
*Things by Richard Bradshaw; the old man is one of a series of images, coping with an increasing load from baby to old age; the figure uses the Greek technique with hinged control rods attached at its back edge, a quick flick while moving it back slightly from the screen reverses the figure to face the opposite way.*

*A hinged control rod, central to the figure, permits manipulation from any angle and enables a good deal of control over the figure even before other rods are added.*

of illumination, some of the controls will often show on the screen, whether clearly or faintly. It is better to accept this as a feature of shadow play rather than to use inadequate controls in an attempt to hide them. The spectator quickly focuses on the figure and forgets the controls.

The main control must be sufficiently strong to cope with the weight of the shadow puppet so that it produces clean movement and does not flex unless you require it to. Its length is determined partly by the methods of operation and lighting as these determine where the operators stand in relation to the screen. It is helpful also if the figure can be held in repose on the screen with the ends of the controls resting on a ledge below the screen. Usually the control rods for a figure are of about the same length.

## Human Figures

These often have one main supporting rod and one or two further controls for moving parts, whether the head, a hand, arm or leg. Some performers use multiple control wires or rods, but this is unusual and unnecessarily cumbersome. In all but the most skilful hands, it will almost certainly detract from the puppet's movements. For the best results keep the controls simple. Let the

puppet's natural movement work for you and add the minimum of controls necessary for the required action. Two or three rods with definite control are far better than a complicated series of rods that is difficult to manage. For some purposes you might have a duplicate figure with controls designed for a particular action rather than try to build a range of functions into a single figure.

Attach the main rod to the body or to a moving head if there is to be no control to the body. The puppet may have a head *and* body control but this is more difficult to operate. A figure may be pivoted at the waist with no direct form of control below it. If leg controls are not used, leg movements are effected indirectly through the manipulation of the main control rod. With just a little practice you will find that you can achieve a surprising range of movements and exert a significant amount of control over the entire figure through the main control rod or wire. Generally the main control rod has a firm attachment, rigid or hinged, so that the puppet responds immediately to any turning of it. By contrast, there will be less strain and damage to moving parts if their controls are attached to them slightly loosely.

A control to the leading hand is the most common addition, sometimes to both hands. With two hand controls

*Two controls operate this figure, cut in card by Jessica Souhami for Shadowstring Theatre; the body and the rear arm are in one piece and, given the shape of the figure, the main control is attached at the shoulder while the forward arm is articulated and has a separate control.*

there will be times when both will be moved together and others when one will hang loosely while the other is operated. However, the weight of the hanging control will restrict the movement of this arm, whereas an arm hanging freely with no control would benefit more from natural movement.

Groups of figures may be attached to a common control with a simple mechanism to move them in unison if necessary, or they may be attached so as to move together but with the limbs free to move independently. Sometimes, when a group is to move together on the screen with independent movements, the figures are suspended from

a horizontal wire that is itself suspended on strong thread(s) or has its ends bent at right angles to form the control.

For human figures and animals that walk upright, attach the main control to a strong part of the figure. If it is of a suitable size, hold the figure lightly between your thumb and forefinger, then gently turn it, letting it return to the upright position by itself. Adjust where you hold it until it turns with the least resistance and resumes the vertical easily. This is the best place at which to attach the main control, with just a little more weight below the control than there is above it. The puppet will now remain naturally upright rather than try to invert itself as you operate it.

85

*St Francis and his horse taking cloth to market, by the Lighthouse Children at Shadowstring Theatre; made from Bextrene, a toughened polystyrene sheet, they are joined to a common base and have two controls to keep them moving smoothly without straining any part.*

## ANIMAL FIGURES

For animals that walk on four legs it is most common to attach the main supporting control to the body at a suitable point for good balance. A secondary control is usually attached to the head. For some purposes, such as a very large animal figure, you might need a control to the front and the rear of the body. Then you would have to decide whether to have a third control to the head, to have the head fixed or to have partial movement of the head, with this restricted but not controlled directly. Where you have a separate head control and two body controls, with practice you can operate two rods with one hand and the third with the other. Alternatively, some performers devise means of loosely linking such controls, for example, with cord or Velcro, to meet the requirements of the situation. Legs normally hang freely, unless a control is needed for a particular action.

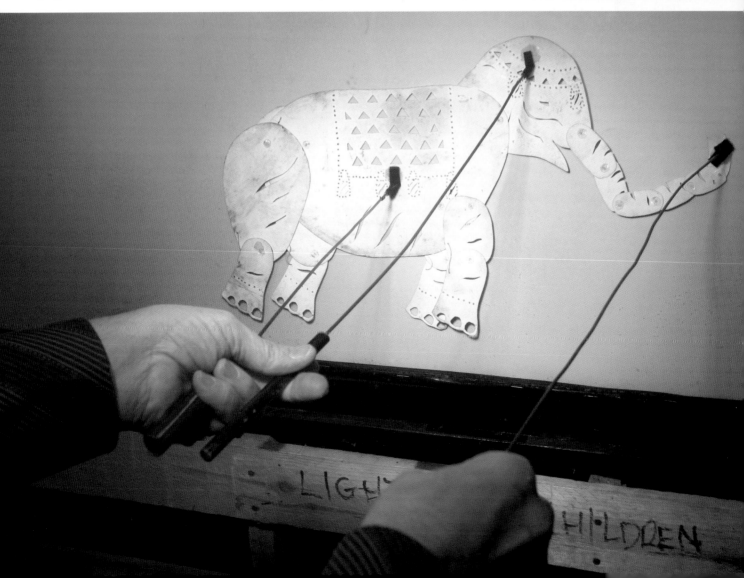

A circus horse and an elephant made by Jessica Souhami from coloured and oiled card for Shadowstring Theatre; the horse requires only two controls while the elephant has a third one for the trunk; Paul Doran holds the head and body rods with one hand, keeping the body control secure in his palm while using his thumb, forefinger and middle finger to move the head.

## METHODS OF FIXING THE MAIN CONTROLS

Control rods may be made from wire, such as 12–14-gauge piano wire or 16-gauge galvanized wire, umbrella ribs, bicycle spokes, metal rods, 8–9mm-diameter softwood dowel rods or strips of card. Dowel rods are thicker than the other types of control and may be more noticeable on the screen. Strips of clear acetate may be used with lightweight figures, but they are generally limited to control from below or with figures laid flat on an overhead projector. Plexiglas strips may be used to control Plexiglas figures, but, in order to achieve good control, these generally need to be thicker (6–10mm, up to nearly ½in) than those used for the shadow figure itself.

To aid manipulation when using any form of control made from wire or thin metal rod, glue the end securely into a hole drilled into a wooden handle made from dowelling (preferably) or bamboo cane (available from garden centres). Make the hole for the wire a very tight fit and ease the wire in with pliers. You might prefer a long wire with a short rod or a shorter wire with a long rod. Regularly check that the wire is secure in the handle.

When connecting the controls, remember to take account of who has to talk to whom and what the action requires so that the control is on the appropriate side of the puppet. Attach the control by one of the following techniques; my own preferences are looped and hinged wire, Velcro or a hinged wooden block.

### Drawing Pin (Thumb Tack)

Secure a dowel rod to the puppet with a drawing pin. Tap it in firmly to prevent the puppet from spinning on the rod. This is suitable only for horizontal controls and is a basic method not used by professionals. After a while, the puppet will develop a hole where the dowel is fixed. It needs to be stored with the rod on a ledge or shelf and with the puppet standing freely over the edge, not laid flat on a surface. However, it is a quick and easy method for introducing children to shadow play.

### Velcro

Glue Velcro tape to the rod and to the puppet. For extra security you may staple the Velcro to the puppet, but ensure that you tap the points in so that they cannot snag the screen. Velcro is suitable for horizontal controls and for puppets up to about 30cm (12in) high. Larger figures will be too heavy for the Velcro to grip. Ensure that you always use one half of the tape (the loops) on the puppet and the other half (the hooks) on the control so that a control can be used with any figure.

With a dowel rod, you may glue the Velcro securely to its circular end. With other controls, such as thin metal rods, glue the Velcro to the end of the shaft. Glue the Velcro

*The control wire is glued securely into a hole in a dowel rod that forms a handle for the control.*

*A simple dowel rod control secured with a drawing pin through the cardboard body.*

*Velcro tape used to join a dowel rod control to a cardboard body.*

around the rod with approximately 2.5cm (1in) extending beyond the end. Keep it curled over, squeeze a little adhesive inside, then squeeze it flat and bend it at right angles to the rod. This should hold its position but allow a little flexibility.

## Eyelet and Toggle

Make a toggle from a thin piece of dowel. Attach it to the main control rod with thin, flexible wire. Use an eyelet punch to fix a suitably sized eyelet in the puppet and insert

the toggle through the eyelet. This method permits control from any angle and, provided that the wire is sufficiently long, enables you to turn the puppet around.

## Looped and Hinged Wire

Make an elongated loop in a piece of wire at right angles to the main shaft. Glue a strip of card or acetate to the puppet over the wire, but not to it, so that the wire can be raised and lowered in the groove in which it sits. This permits you to

*Velcro is glued to a control rod and the end is flattened to provide a flexible attachment to a shadow puppet cut from X-ray film; Shadowstring Theatre.*

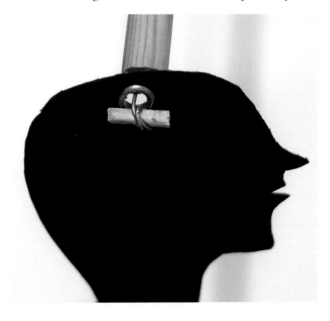

*A toggle and eyelet joint for a control.*

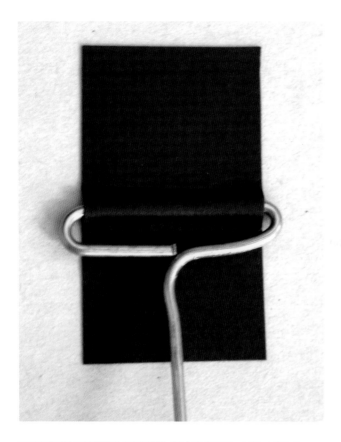

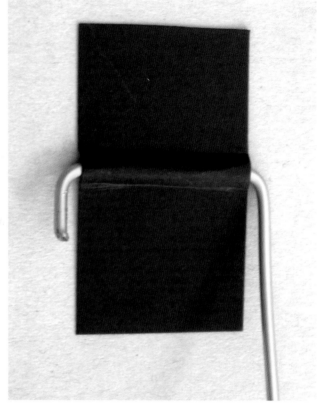

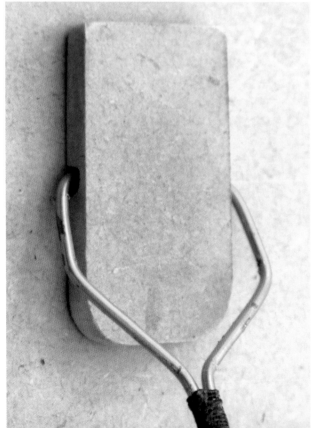

*ABOVE LEFT: A looped wire control hinged to the figure with a strip of card.*
*ABOVE: A square-cornered, 'U'-shaped control hinged to the figure with a strip of card.*
*LEFT: A looped wire control attached by a grooved wooden block.*

operate from any angle and is an extremely quick and effective method. As an alternative to the loop of wire, bend the wire into a sharp-angled 'U' shape with one long and one short end. With the full-loop method the long control wire is central to the hinge and therefore well-balanced. If you use the alternative method, adjust the attachment point as necessary to achieve this balance.

To adopt the looped wire method with a plywood puppet, use thicker wire and replace the cardboard retainer with a grooved piece of wood. Glue and, if necessary, screw the block to the plywood figure, ensuring that the wire turns freely in the groove. Bend the long and the short end of the wire back and bind them together, but ensure that they are sufficiently clear of the wooden block so as not to restrict the movement of the wire.

## Hinged Wooden Block

This method is suitable for plywood figures that need a strong main control rod. I adopted it after seeing it used so effectively at the Little Angel Theatre in London. For the main control use an 8mm (⁵⁄₁₆in) wooden dowel rod. Glue the rod securely into a hole drilled in the square end of a wedge-shaped block of wood of 32mm (1¼in) square section. Use a hinge screwed to the sloping face of the block to attach it to a thinner block that is glued and, if necessary, screwed to a suitable point on the figure.

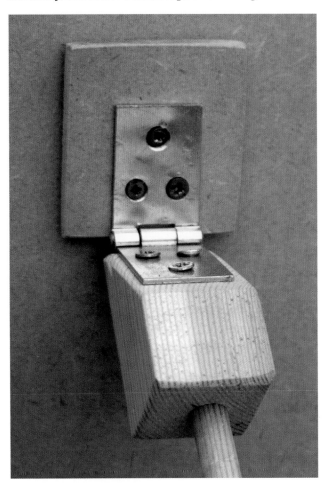

## Steel Rod

For a strong, fine control, a thin steel rod is a good choice and is especially suitable for attachment to the edge of a figure to enable it to be turned around. Bend fine galvanized wire into a 'U' shape to fit on to the end of the rod, with a small loop protruding at the end. Bind the loop to the rod with a fine wire, such as fuse wire, and solder it into place. Sand or file the surface as necessary to create a smooth finish. Use thread to attach the fine wire loop to the reinforced edge of the figure. A small piece of acetate is useful for the reinforcement.

## Umbrella Spoke

The frames from old umbrellas, especially large golf umbrellas, are a popular choice for use with lighter puppets because of their combination of strength and modest

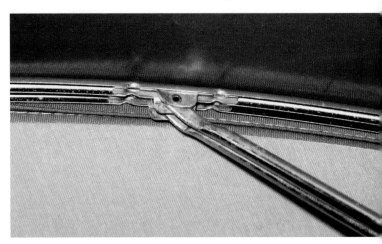

LEFT: *A wooden block with a brass hinge is used to attach the dowel control rod to a plywood figure.*
ABOVE: *The spokes from a large umbrella are useful for shadow puppet controls.*
BELOW: *Thin, galvanized wire is bound with fine wire to the end of a steel rod and soldered in place; the small loop at the end is used to attach the rod to the reinforced edge of a shadow figure.*

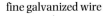

fine galvanized wire          fuse wire binding

steel model wire

RIGHT: *An umbrella spoke with the joint intact is attached securely and centrally to this shadow puppet, by Steve and Chris Clarke for Shadowstring Theatre.*
BELOW: *This figure, from a Japanese legend by Caricature Theatre for television, is an example of puppeteers' inventiveness. The control rod was attached to this figure using the white holder salvaged from another application; the joints were made with studs that are used to attach plastic letters for signage.*

thickness; they also have useful pre-drilled holes. While you would remove just a single spoke to use for a hand or leg control, for a main control it is often better to remove an entire joint, including a short length of the wire that forms the frame of the dome. Leave a little protruding on each side of the joint, to create a 'T'-shape with the main spoke. Attach the wire to the puppet at a suitable point. The nature of the figure determines how you should do this. Three methods are suggested but you might invent your own to meet your particular needs. Ensure that the attachment is secure and able to fold flat for packing.

Attach the control with a suitable, strong glue.

Pierce small holes in the figure where the control is to be joined and insert fine wires or strong thread through these holes, twist or knot them over the small remaining protrusions that are attached to the joint with the spoke.

Glue a strip of card over the wire on each side of the joint, ensure that the spoke is free to rotate in order for you to be able to change the angle of the control.

Finally, glue the end of the spoke into a dowelling handle, as described above.

## ARM CONTROLS

It is possible, but not common, to dispense with arm controls and let the arms hang and move freely, particularly if the arms are cut in an interesting position rather than dangling limply. However, with some large figures it is not uncommon for the puppeteer to pick up the hand and simply hold it against the screen – and it works.

## Rod or Wire

The best all-purpose method for controlling arms from behind or below requires a thin rod or wire, particularly an umbrella spoke or galvanized wire. Make use of the pre-drilled hole in an umbrella spoke or make a loop in the end of a piece of wire and seal the closure of the loop with glue. Use strong thread to tie the control to the hand, but not too tightly or it might damage the puppet during use. With puppets made from a strong material you might attach the control with fine wire. Ensure that the control is able to move freely in all directions. Alternatively glue Velcro to the control and to the limb to join them.

## Acetate

Attach a strip of strong, clear acetate to the hand with thread knotted at each side of the joint. This method and the next are suitable only for control from below.

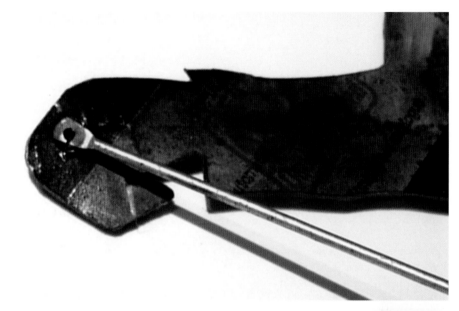

*RIGHT: An umbrella spoke attached to a thin plywood hand with fine wire.*
*BELOW: A hand control made from galvanized wire is attached to the hand with strong thread; the loop in the wire is sealed with glue.*
*BELOW RIGHT: A Velcro spot can be used to attach a control rod tipped with the corresponding piece of Velcro.*

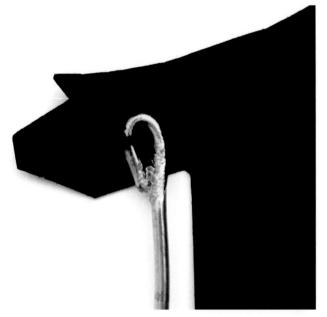

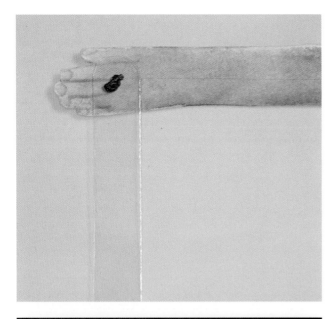

## String

Extend the top of the arm beyond the pivot to create leverage and attach a string to it to raise the arm. The longer the extension, the more leverage it will give and the smoother the movement will tend to be. The weight of the arm acts as a counter-pull but, to ensure controlled movement, fix a piece of elastic between the arm and the body.

## LEG CONTROLS

### Indirect Control

Some performers avoid leg controls unless they are absolutely necessary, allowing the legs to hang and move freely. The decision may be determined by the nature of the performance – the more lively and humorous the item, the less you might want leg controls, whereas more restrained or refined action might require very definite leg control, but this is not a rule. You can achieve a good deal of leg control through the momentum of the whole figure and by gently swinging or rocking the main control with a slight downward pressure.

### Wire and Acetate Controls

For a highly controlled leg action, connect a piece of galvanized wire, an umbrella spoke or a strip of strong, clear acetate to the foot with knotted thread or a loop of fine wire. Often a figure is constructed with one leg articulated and the other fixed. Attach the main control wire to the figure and an extra wire to the articulated leg. Turning the main control will cause the puppet to stoop forward slightly and then straighten up as it walks.

*TOP: An acetate hand control.*
*ABOVE: Extending the top of an arm provides leverage for attaching a vertical control string.*
*RIGHT: An umbrella spoke attached to a plywood foot with a loop of wire.*

## MOVING HEAD

When a figure has a moving head, the main control may be attached to it rather than to the body, but it is preferable to use separate controls for the head and the body. Make the control to the body the main support and the head control the subsidiary one. Attach the controls by one of the methods described previously.

## MOVING MOUTH

A moving mouth may be designed with the head fixed and the lower jaw moving or the chin fixed and the top of the head moving. It may be controlled by a piece of wire or a pull-string, with elastic used as a counter-pull to return it to its original position. Usually the elastic is used to hold the mouth closed but occasionally may hold it open with the string used to close it. You might need strips of card or a thin strip of wood glued to the figure at suitable points to limit the range of movement.

An ingenious traditional device used for some eastern figures is a slender and springy piece of wood attached horizontally high in the head. A fine thread is used to join the mouth to this strip, which flexes downwards when a pull-string opens the mouth. As soon as the tension is

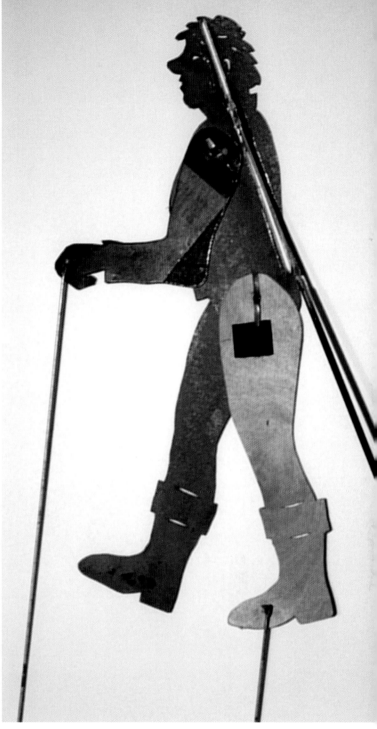

ABOVE: *This puppet, by Steve and Chris Clarke for Shadowstring Theatre, has one leg articulated and separately controlled while the other one is cut as a fixed part of the figure; as the articulated leg moves forward, the figure stoops slightly and then straightens up as the fixed leg moves forward.*
LEFT: *The moving mouth of this Thai puppet is operated by a pull-thread with a rubber band as a counter-pull.*

*A BURMESE SHADOW PUPPET WITH A MOVING MOUTH.*
OPPOSITE PAGE: *The full figure – the moving mouth is operated by thread with a counter-pull from a flexible, thin strip of wood attached level with the forehead.* BELOW: *Detail of the lever, attached to a slot in the control, to produce mouth movements.*

RIGHT: *The owl, from* Witch Is Which *by Shadowstring Theatre, is made of acetate and operated by a main control rod, attached with Velcro, a string uses leverage to move the wings in jumping jack-style.*

released the strip of wood returns to its original position, closing the mouth.

## CONTROL STRINGS

Any strings used to control shadow puppets will usually be quite fine but should not stretch, kink, fray or break easily. I favour a strong thread, such as Dacron braided nylon fishing line.

### Combining Strings and Rods

Control strings may be used in conjunction with rods operated vertically from below or from an angle. Control strings tend to be used in two main ways described below:

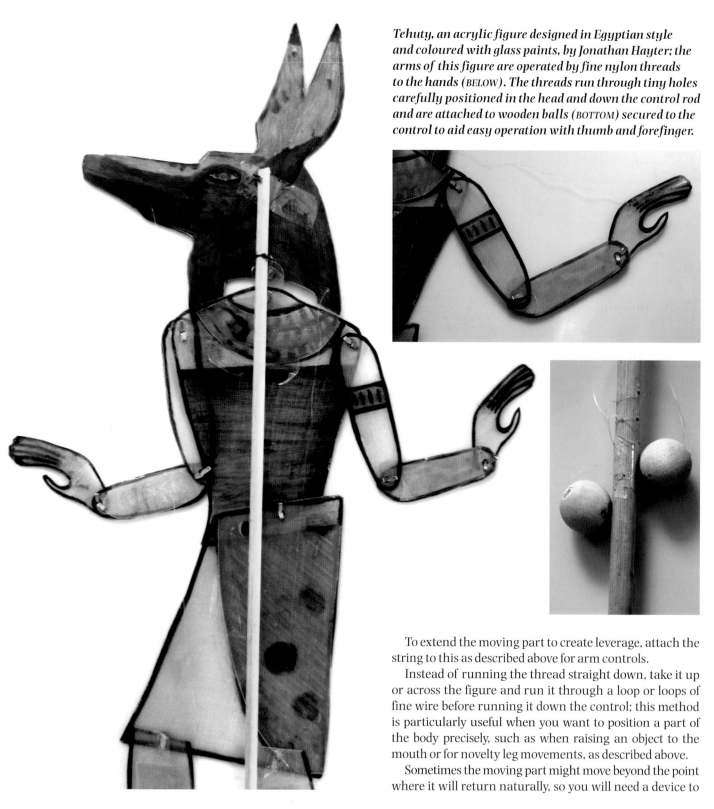

*Tehuty, an acrylic figure designed in Egyptian style and coloured with glass paints, by Jonathan Hayter; the arms of this figure are operated by fine nylon threads to the hands (BELOW). The threads run through tiny holes carefully positioned in the head and down the control rod and are attached to wooden balls (BOTTOM) secured to the control to aid easy operation with thumb and forefinger.*

To extend the moving part to create leverage, attach the string to this as described above for arm controls.

Instead of running the thread straight down, take it up or across the figure and run it through a loop or loops of fine wire before running it down the control; this method is particularly useful when you want to position a part of the body precisely, such as when raising an object to the mouth or for novelty leg movements, as described above.

Sometimes the moving part might move beyond the point where it will return naturally, so you will need a device to

98

*LEFT: Spiders cut from X-ray film by Paul Doran; one is suspended on thread while the other has a control rod attached with Velcro.*
*RIGHT: A crossbar along the base of the screen assists manipulation.*

limit the degree of movement or to act as a counter-pull. Use a restricting piece of thread, a block of wood or card, or a piece of elastic to serve this purpose.

Any control string must be easy to identify during performance, especially if there is more than one string, and so a small coloured bead on each string will be useful both for quick identification and as a means to operate it with pressure on the bead by your thumb or finger. Where there is more than one string try to separate them slightly as they run down the puppet. This will aid the clean operation of the correct string.

## SUSPENDED PUPPETS

You can also suspend a shadow puppet on strings. Attach it to a control that may be very simple, like a makeshift fishing rod with a single string or horizontal rods to which a number of strings are fixed. However, you need to take care about where you are positioned if your own shadow is not to show.

A strong source of light is essential if you require sharp shadows because a suspended figure will not be pressed tightly against the screen. Consequently, this method is rarely used other than to fulfil a particular need.

## OPERATING METHODS

This section deals with the elemental techniques for operating controls (*see also* the chapter on performance, page 179, for advice on manipulation).

Normally each puppet requires one operator. Only with very simple figures will you be able to hold one with each hand. Control through the main rod is helped by the rhythm of the operation and the momentum of the whole figure, the turning of the rod, gentle pressure against the screen and the use of a base strip for the figures to walk on.

When operating more than two rods, the method to be used depends on the function of these rods and what is most comfortable for you. For example, you might hold the main supporting rod in one hand and use the other to operate two rods for limbs or a head and a limb. When operating rods to the head, body and two hands, you might find the best technique is to hold the main supporting (body) rod in the palm of one hand while using the thumb and first two fingers of the same hand to manipulate the head rod. The other hand controls both hand rods.

When operating the main rod plus a hand and a leg, you might find it helpful to hold the main rod and the hand rod in one hand, using your thumb and first two fingers to manipulate the hand rod. Use you other hand to manipulate the leg rod. Alternatively, you might pair up the body and leg controls and keep your free hand for the hand control. When one hand needs to operate two control rods, such as for the body and an arm, it is sometimes useful to link the handles of the controls together loosely. This allows one rod to hang freely at times and for you to resume control easily when required. It also helps the less experienced operator to avoid dropping it completely. To link the controls, drill holes through each of the handles; thread a piece of cord through each and knot the ends. Ensure that the cord allows sufficient movement of each part but also allows the one hanging freely to be picked up easily.

When a figure has any additional control(s), especially a figure made from card, take care not to pull the controls too vigorously in different directions. This could result in the control breaking away or causing a dismembered hand, arm or leg. Some materials might be reinforced if very vigorous action is required.

Companies using complex figures may require two operators to a single puppet. This is not very practicable with small puppets, although occasionally you might need a helping hand for a particular manoeuvre. Remember that two operators need much more space to move in backstage than the puppet needs on the screen. The puppeteers must also rehearse thoroughly so that they can work with coordinated timing and avoid straining the figure by pressure in different directions. For larger figures operated from below like rod puppets, any rhythmic movement of the operator is transferred to the movement of the puppet. An added dimension may be achieved by the choice of material for the supporting rod, such as the use of spring steel since springy wire tends to make a puppet quiver as it moves.

If you were in Java and needed more figures on screen than there were operators you would have a banana plant placed behind the screen and the sharpened ends of the

**PAUL DORAN MANIPULATING SHADOW FIGURES IN THREE WAYS.**
*ABOVE LEFT: Two control rods held separately.*
*LEFT: Two rods are held in one hand when a free one is needed for a third rod or another action.*
*ABOVE: Operating the main control and a leg with one hand and the puppet's arm with the other one.*

rods would be stuck firmly into it. In the west we would generally adopt one of three possible solutions:

- Create a group of duplicate figures cut in one piece with some moving parts that you can operate.
- Allow the figures that are not so involved in the action to rest in repose against the screen with their rods supported on a ledge behind the screen (*see* page 112).
- Construct a 'repose bar' (*see* image below and page 111) and cover it with Velcro; cover the wooden handles of the control rods with the corresponding Velcro to hold them securely in place on the bar.

Shadow puppets that need to be held tightly against the screen cannot easily pass one another on stage, although this is an area in which figures operated vertically have a slight advantage over those operated at an angle. You might decide to withdraw one figure from the screen and simply replace it on the other side of the figure it is passing. Alternatively, you can allow the figures to cross one another by raising one slightly so that it clears the other puppet; this is probably the more common way of handling the cross-over. Practise this manoeuvre until it is so smooth that you do not drop the puppets or have them collide.

If you are a solo performer, having figures crossing in this way means that you are operating with your arms crossed, so practise ways of exchanging the rods smoothly from one hand to the other as you effect the cross-over. With two or more operators you need to negotiate whether you:

- cross one another with one crouching down to allow the other to pass,
- pass the puppet to the next operator to use, or
- pass the puppet along and then move past that person to retrieve your puppet.

Different circumstances will require different solutions.

Processions may need two carefully positioned control rods in order for it to be possible to support and move the group, and, if the legs dangle freely, they will move in time with one another or individually, depending on the rhythm of your operation.

I offer two additional pieces of advice:

- if rods are fixed horizontally, when a character is not on screen, rest the rods on a flat surface with the figures over the edge so that they do not bend or suffer damage, and
- always have a spare rod handy in case it is needed during the performance; it is useful if this has a hooked end so that it can be used in several ways (you might have one with a Velcro end too, if this is your method of attaching controls), the rod is used to perform additional operations, as needed, or it might be a standby to help if technical hitches arise.

*A control rest for figures in repose on one of Paul Doran's shadow stages; the repose bar and the handles of the controls are covered with corresponding strips of Velcro so that the figures are held securely in place when the handles are pressed on to the bar.*

# 7 STAGING

## STAGING PRINCIPLES

The stages described in this chapter provide a basis on which you can design your own for different performances, because your staging needs may change with the nature of the performance. Some performers will require a taut

*OPPOSITE PAGE:*
*Backstage at a performance by Theatre-en-Ciel.*

*THIS PAGE:*
*Staging for Apollo Workshop, an art & science project linked to Moontime by Jonathan Hayter, Figure of Speech.*

screen in a traditional framework with curtains to hide all backstage activity. Others may have a different performance concept, with different types of screen and no need to hide themselves as they perform. This chapter describes staging and screens that lend themselves to both types of approach. They are among the most flexible and useful that I have used or that have been used by other shadow players, and provide a good selection to draw upon.

Always ensure that your staging is presentable, strong, rigid and stable. Remember that the figures may be pressed quite firmly against it. You will probably need it to be portable, easy to assemble and dismantle, and it must accommodate the performers as well as the puppets. Consider also how you will transport and store it.

Contemporary explorations with staging are described in a later chapter (*see* pages 168–170).

## THE SCREEN

The size and the shape of a screen and the way in which it is framed establish the nature of the acting area.

### Size, Position and Tension
Screens vary in size from 1m to 10m wide (3–33ft) and from 75cm to 5m (30in–16ft) high. A traditional Chinese screen would be approximately 1.5m (5ft) wide and 1m high. A large fabric screen has a greater tendency to give when a figure is pressed against it, especially towards the centre, which can cause other figures to lose definition. If you require a large screen, consider how you will light it if you want to achieve an even illumination.

The height of the screen from the floor depends upon the demands of the performance, the method of control, the type of lighting to be used and the heights of the performers. You should also consider the types of venue in which your performance is to be given and therefore the sight lines of the audience.

It is useful if the shadow screen can be tilted slightly with the top towards the audience. This helps figures and scenery to remain flat against a taut screen rather than tending to fall away from it. It is also helpful to have a ledge behind and below the screen to hold the rods of figures in repose. Varying the tension of the screen between taut and free-flowing (*see* page 168) adds another significant dimension to the visual picture and the nature of the performance.

## Shape

Traditionally, the landscape-orientated screen has been the most common type and clearly this lends itself to mainly horizontal movement. The proportions of such screens range from the traditional (height two-thirds of the width) to processional (height approximately half the width) or somewhere in between. Circular screens are sometimes used purely for horizontal movement for small cameo items alongside a larger screen, but a large circular screen facilitates action around the circumference, as well as in and from all directions. Vertical screens are less common but are ideal for vertical movement.

A wide variety of shapes is used for different performances, but, for greater flexibility, it is often better

*ABOVE*: *A city landscape from* No Trees No Life, *created with black card and coloured, self-adhesive film on acetate in pageant or processional dimensions at the Shadowstring Theatre.*
*LEFT*: *'Traditional' proscenium-shaped scenery for* The Snow Queen *by Jane Phillips's Caricature Theatre; an additional circular mask was added to project a 3m image on to a screen as a background for three-dimensional figures.*

to keep to a limited number of basic shapes and use masking inserts or projections to establish particular shapes or even to change them during a performance, as described in the chapter on scenery (page 124). The flexible staging units described on pages 115–121 allow for considerable flexibility in exchanging screens for different performances.

Screens can also be constructed to represent objects, either for the whole performance or as a side-screen within one, so that the action is seen as if through a car window, the windows of a house or even inside a clock face. In one production some of the action took place inside a head, showing the character's thoughts, memories and ideas. Another divided a large circle into segments in which the action took place, with the circle revolving at given moments.

## Masking

Generally a shadow theatre needs sufficient masked space at the sides of the screen to cover figures, props or scenery as they enter or leave the screen, as well as screening below, and often above, the playing area in order that the performers should not be seen, if this is your intention.

## SINGLE AND MULTIPLE SCREENS

For traditional fixed screens you might have a single one for all purposes or a number of them, each with its own lighting. The single screen might have cut-out scenery that is physically changed for each scene or projected scenery that fades from one image to the next. Alternatively, with fast moving scenes, you could divide the entire screen into

*ABOVE: A frame for a circular projection of* **The Cat That Walked by Himself** *by the DaSilva Puppet Company; the frame is 60cm square and the projected image is over 150cm in diameter, the frames are carefully numbered for smooth transitions during the performance.*

*BELOW: This screen is divided to create two areas for different parts of the action, either consecutively or simultaneously.*
*BELOW RIGHT: Multiple screens in different shapes, sizes and heights designed for use together in one performance.*

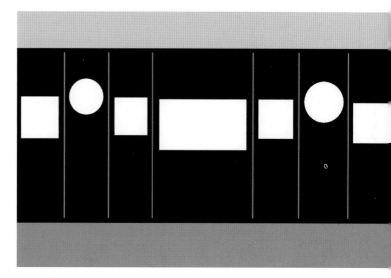

compartments for different parts of the action that might happen consecutively or simultaneously.

A stage might have multiple screens in any shape, size, height or arrangement. If necessary, some screens might have a raised platform for the performers, but ensure that it is of suitable dimensions so that the players can step backwards without falling off.

If you are using multiple screens, you may or may not be concerned about the possibility of the light for one screen spilling on to another, particularly if that screen is not in use. If this is an issue, you must either direct, and possibly shield, the light carefully or have a means of shielding the screen, such as drapes or internal shutters, when it is not in use.

An unusual arrangement of screens, set out in several orientations to create shadows of the same object on different surfaces is described in the chapter on contemporary approaches (*see* pages 169–170).

## COMBINING SHADOWS AND THREE-DIMENSIONAL PUPPETS

If shadow puppets are used in conjunction with three-dimensional puppets, there are many ways of arranging the screen. For example, it may be:

- set to the side, or on each side, of the acting area,
- suspended above the stage and raised and lowered with cords and pulleys,
- hinged and raised and lowered between the horizontal and the vertical position,
- fixed on a trolley-type frame and wheeled on and off stage,
- built into the stage as a backcloth,
- inserted into a proscenium opening, or
- built into the front frame of a stage, above or below the other puppets' acting area.

A larger screen may be used to present human shadows, possibly masked. If required, these may be combined with shadow puppets on the same screen or on a separate screen of appropriate size.

## STORAGE

Store your screen carefully, especially if it is made from a rigid material that could be scratched and permanently marked. I store mine in a box with a protective material on each side of the screen itself. You could use, for example, large sheets of strong card, some type of fairly rigid plastic foam sheet (my choice) or bubble wrap. It may be useful to keep the packaging in which a rigid screen is purchased.

## MATERIAL FOR THE SCREEN

In presenting shadows a great deal will depend on the quality of the screen used. Shadow screens must transmit as much light as possible, but, at the same time, be sufficiently opaque to hide the puppeteers. For traditional shadow play it needs to be taut so that the puppets can be pushed against it lightly without its sagging but thin enough to give sharp edges to the shadows. It usually needs to be strong and durable too. Make the screen from a reasonably strong, semi-opaque material, for which you have a wide range of choices. They are arranged below in an approximate order of preference, starting with the most basic and finishing with the highest quality, although this order might change in relation to different applications, the size required and the type of lighting used:

- white cotton, or polyester-cotton, sheeting,
- plain white window-blind material,
- plain white shower curtain fabric,
- architects' tracing film,
- a lighting acetate known as 'frost',
- sailcloth,
- a translucent acrylic sheet, or
- rear-screen projection material.

Polyester-cotton is quite satisfactory but can appear grainy because of the weave, although sometimes a slight texture might suit your purposes. I find the finish and smoothness of a plain shower curtain preferable and it transmits light very evenly.

Architects' tracing sheet or matt plastic drafting film is excellent for colour transmission. 50-micron double matt drafting film is good but 75-micron film is much stronger. Take care not to purchase versions with a slight colour tint.

A 'frost' acetate will be stronger than drafting film but needs careful handling to avoid its being scratched. Acetate and similar sheets usually come with a protective film on the surface. This may look perfect for shadow play but the film marks easily and allows pinpoints of intense light through the surface so it has to be peeled off. Its rigidity may be a factor when considering transportation, with the additional bulk of an adequate protective covering.

*RIGHT*: **The Circus:**
*The Ostrich on
a tightrope, by Richard
Bradshaw; Richard now
prefers to use a rigid screen
which is a transparent,
acrylic sheet, 1 to 2 mm
thick, with a non-reflective
surface on the audience
side.*
*BELOW*: *For this screen Paul
Doran uses sailcloth
stretched over an acetate
sheet; puppets and scenery
were cut in card and X-ray
film.*

*A textured appearance may be achieved by the fabric of the screen itself or by projection; Hastings by La Citrouille, France.*

A rigid acrylic sheet, approximately 1.2mm thick and used with the non-reflective surface facing the audience, is now the preferred choice of Richard Bradshaw.

Sailcloth is excellent if it is available in sufficient width (purchase it from ships' chandlers). Paul Doran (Shadowstring Theatre) has used sailcloth stretched across an acetate sheet and this combination worked extremely well.

Rear-screen projection material is excellent for multiple light effects and projection methods with colourful figures; it is available in different finishes, the choice of which will be influenced by the type of performance and lighting methods. Roscoscreen, for example, is available in seven finishes, five of which are good for shadow play. Front White is too dense and Light Translucent too transparent, but Black, Grey, Twin White, Misty Blue and Sky Blue transmit colours effectively. The main difference between them with the lights typically used for shadow play is the slightly different tint each gives to the plain parts of the screen when illuminated and their appearance when not illuminated. When illuminated, Misty Blue looks white, Sky Blue almost as white, Twin White is somewhat creamy, Grey is almost white and Black looks slightly grey. With these considerations I tend towards Misty Blue, but the appearance of the staging for a particular performance

might indicate a different choice. All except Black may be purchased by the metre in 1.4 or 2.2m (4½ or 7ft) widths, which are sufficient for most performers' needs. A 2.8m (9ft) width is available but has a join because it is made from two 1.4m widths. Black is available only in 1.4m and 2.8m widths. Individual screens can also be made up, with a join, in any size you specify, with a raw edge, plain seam or seam with eyelets or piped pockets.

The suggestions above do not constitute an exhaustive list. The screen may be made from any one of a host of materials or, indeed, sometimes from a mixture of materials, including sacking, gauze or cheesecloth to give texture to the scene and the figures. A mixture of materials, such as sacking with a cotton insert or vice versa, allows the audience to see not only the shadows but the actual figures through the weave of the sacking. Another technique to make both shadows and figures visible is to have a screen with a cut-out section or sections. Even a large parasol may be used for a screen.

## STAGE CONSTRUCTION

### Basic Stages
Shadow play can be performed with very simple staging, such as a screen and curtains attached to a three-sided

clothes horse. The screen may be pinned in an open doorway, although this is usually an inconvenient arrangement. Large cardboard boxes are easily opened out and a shape cut-out to accommodate a screen that is taped on. A picture frame is quickly turned into a shadow theatre, with a top cross bar to hold side curtains and wooden 'feet' attached by brackets for support.

A domestic garment rail provides a framework for a large screen, for example, with a plain white shower curtain. It is quickly assembled and dismantled, lightweight and strong. However, of all these arrangements, only the picture frame and the garment rail come close to offering a reasonably stable screen and even this may be quite limited in size, proportions and strength.

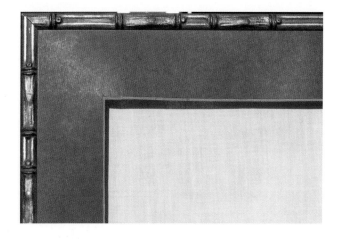

*ABOVE: A picture frame used to hold a cotton shadow screen.*

*LEFT: A domestic garment rail used to hang a shower curtain for shadow play; the screen may be used taut, slack or in folds.*

109

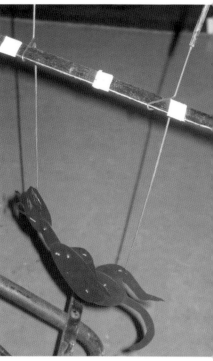

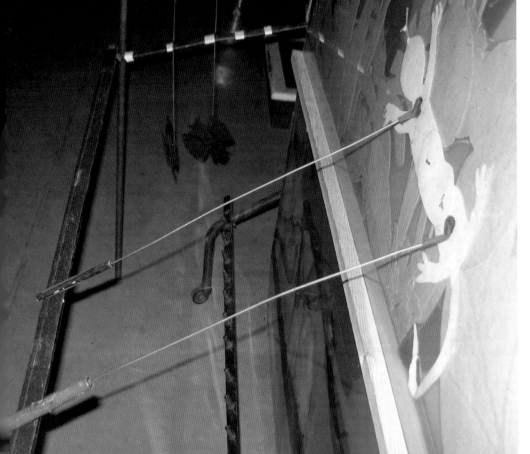

## Purpose-built Stages

For modest applications it is advisable to construct your own table-top screen, which is very similar to a picture frame with good support and masking screens. More ambitious productions may require individual designs or you can use the flexible staging units described below. These can be rearranged in various orientations and you can construct additional features if required.

Shadow players often create their own alternative structures to fit the design concept of the production and they are quite inventive with large stages that need to fit into available transport. Examples include incorporating a large, commercial garment rail or taping the top of the screen to fairly large (for example, 10cm diameter) aluminium tubing so that the screen can be rolled up safely without creasing; the bottom is attached to another tube or to the wooden frame of the stage.

One of Paul Doran's shadow stages is constructed on a large garment rail with a variety of additions to aid easy access to puppets, including two types of control rest to hold the figures off stage during a performance and a bar to hold figures in repose on the screen. One is a wooden bar fixed between the legs of the stand; the bar has protruding dowel pegs that hold the controls in place while the figure rests on the floor (which needs to be clean) in front of the performers; a second long bar extends the length of the screen a short distance behind and below it, its surface is covered with Velcro tape and the wooden handles of the puppet controls are covered with the corresponding tape

so that they will grip on the bar to hold figures in repose. This bar is held clear of the screen by two wooden side battens, all parts being bolted together so that they can be swivelled aside when not in use. The battens serve a double purpose as they also hold the puppets when off screen; to assist this, each control rod has a loop made near the handle so that it can slip securely on to the side battens.

The surrounds of the screen are usually masked with a set of flats or with curtains arranged on a wooden framework. Ensure that the material will not let light show through unless you intend it to.

Some performances require a portable screen. A simple framework can be supported on wheels (or casters) with locking mechanisms, or on wheels at one end and blocks of wood at the other, to prevent it from moving unintentionally.

## ATTACHING THE SCREEN

There is no rule about whether to attach the screen to the operators' or the audience's side of the framework. If the screen is attached to the audience side of the frame, the lower cross-bar provides a convenient ledge upon which puppets can walk, but this will not work if the controls are vertical and the figure must be held against the screen, for which you need the screen on the operators' side.

The means by which you attach the screen to the frame and keep it taut depends partly upon the type of material it is made of. Drawing pins, staples and strong camera tape are

*OPPOSITE PAGE:*

*TOP LEFT: A commercial-sized garment rail with numerous additions was used as the basis for one of Paul Doran's shadow theatres.*

*TOP RIGHT: A control rest for figures off-stage.*

*BOTTOM LEFT: A control rest covered in Velcro for figures in repose on the screen; notice the additional side bar at the far end to hold characters off-stage.*

*MIDDLE AND BOTTOM RIGHT: Detail of the side-bar holding figures off stage; the loops in the control wires hook on to the side bar, the white tape bindings prevent excessive movement of the controls.*

*THIS PAGE:*
*Cord looped through eyelets and over the frame of the stage is a good way to adjust and maintain the tension of a fabric shadow screen.*

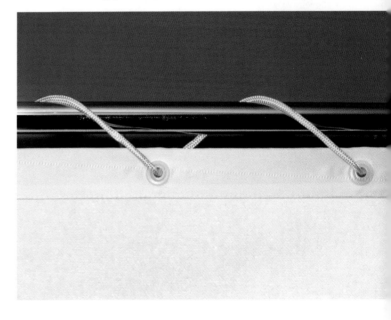

all used, but, for larger stages with a strong material, the best method uses brass eyelets and cord. Create a strong hem all around the screen and evenly space the eyelets in the entire hem at a maximum of 10cm (4in) intervals. Thread strong cord through the eyelets and either around the frame itself or through large screw-eyes in the frame. Tie the ends of the cord together securely to hold the screen taut with an even tension all around.

## A LEDGE FOR CHARACTERS IN REPOSE

One type of repose bar is described above in the description of one of Paul Doran's stages. An alternative ledge is made from a strip of plywood or MDF. It is attached to the main frame in the form of a shelf that runs the length of the screen and just below it. Cover the ledge with a strip of material that will grip the controls; foam rubber or rubber

underlay for carpets are ideal. For added security, glue a narrow wooden batten to the edge of the ledge to prevent the controls from slipping off.

A table-top screen is best used with a suitably sized piece of plywood or MDF placed behind the screen and covered with a strip of material as described above.

## A TABLE-TOP STAGE

Although this stage is described for shadow play, it is very versatile: covering the shadow screen with curtains enables it to be used from behind for glove and rod puppets or, with the puppeteer standing behind it at the level of the base, as a back-screen for marionettes.

The dimensions of the stage depend on the needs of your performance and transport. A suggested minimum screen size is 100cm (40in) wide by 70cm (28in) high;

*THIS PAGE:*
*Richard Bradshaw's early shadow screen, with the ledge to hold characters in repose or to assist the solo performer who has only his or her hands to operate all the figures.*

*OPPOSITE PAGE:*
**A TABLE-TOP STAGE CONSTRUCTED IN WOOD.**
TOP LEFT: *The basic stage with the top cross bar to support the side curtains.*
TOP RIGHT: *A half-lap joint.*
MIDDLE LEFT: *Two lengths of timber are glued and screwed to the base of the stage to ensure a snug fit to hold the frame of the screen.*
MIDDLE RIGHT: *The frame of the screen is inserted in the base and an additional length of timber is bolted on to provide a fixture for the bottom of the screen and a ledge for the puppets to walk on.*
BOTTOM LEFT: *The top cross-bar is held in place by dowel pegs that fit into holes in the main frame.*
BOTTOM RIGHT: *The top cross-bar may be secured further by a hook over a screw and hinged, if necessary, for packing or storage.*

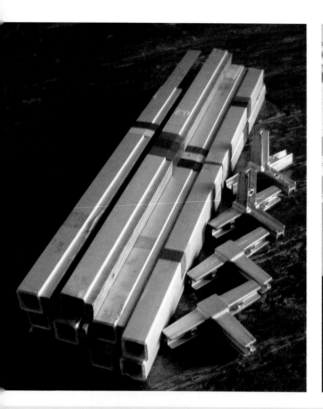

*A small bundle of square-section, aluminium tubing makes up into an alternative form of the table-top stage; coloured tape helps in the identification of the parts for quick assembly.*

120cm×85cm (48in×33in) is better but 150cm×100cm (60in×40in) gives you much more scope if you can accommodate it. For strength and rigidity use 50mm× 25mm (2in×1in) timber for the frame, 18mm chipboard or MDF for the base, and dowelling of approximately 9mm diameter for joining the curtain rail. Use woodworking glue as the adhesive.

The frame for the screen is four lengths of timber, glued and screwed together at right angles with half-lap joints. It is held upright by the base board. Glue and screw two lengths of timber to the base board, using the bottom of the frame as a spacer, countersink the holes for the screw-heads so that the frame will not scratch any surface on which it stands. Insert the frame into the slot in the base; this should be sufficient to hold it securely. If it is necessary to secure it further, drill holes across the assembled base and frame, insert bolts into the holes and fasten with wing nuts.

Use another length of timber for a lower cross-bar. Place it on the rear strip that holds the frame and drill a hole centrally through each end of the cross-bar and the two uprights. You join the cross-bar to the frame with bolts and wing nuts after you attach the shadow screen to the frame. Staple, pin or tape the shadow screen to the top and sides of the frame, taking care to achieve an even tension and a smooth, wrinkle-free surface.

On the audience side of the frame, insert the bolts for the lower cross-bar and cut neat holes in the edges of the screen for the bolts to pass through. Replace the lower cross-bar over the bolts, pull the screen under it tightly and secure it to the side facing the operator. Once again snip neat holes for the bolts to pass through the edge of the screen and add the wing nuts.

This cross-bar provides a ledge on which shadow puppets can walk and the space between screen and cross-bar can be used to hold scenery. The screen can be attached directly to all sides of the frame without attaching it to the lower cross-bar in this way, but the recommended method keeps the screen tighter to the cross-bar and prevents inserted scenery from dropping down too far.

Construct the top cross-bar from two lengths of timber, joined with a strong hinge so that it can be folded up for packing. Position the cross-bar in place on top of the frame and clamp it securely. Drill four well-spaced, 9mm-diameter holes down though the entire bar and frame. Glue four 9mm-diameter dowel pegs, each 7.5cm long (3in), into the holes in the bar so that they protrude downwards to fit into the holes in the frame. The cross-bar is held in place by its weight, but a small hook may be used for extra security.

Curtains are suspended from the cross-bar with Velcro or by means of a curtain wire or rail. A curtain rail with a cording set provides smooth operation for revealing and covering the shadow screen.

A similar table-top stage can be made with aluminium square-section tubing, described on page 119. It is quickly assembled or dismantled to form a small pack of tubes. In order to attach curtains and a shadow screen, screw wooden battens to the tubing with self-tapping screws.

## FLEXIBLE STAGING UNITS

### Design

A set of staging units that can be joined in a variety of configurations can be an economical way to create a larger shadow theatre, which, like the table-top stage, can be used for presenting other types of puppet too if you replace the shadow screen, or you can use it for shadow play in conjunction with other forms of puppet theatre.

A set of flats or hinged units (book flats) can be assembled in minutes, especially if they are joined with pin hinges rather than bolts with wing nuts, and this gives a flexibility of stage design. You can construct the flats or units in a variety of shapes and sizes, but keeping to certain standard sizes offers wider possibilities for rearrangement. Non-standard units can be added at any time.

The units may be anything up to 2.5m (8ft) high, but if they are to be transported you may need them to be much smaller. My own set is made up of two main sizes: hinged units are 90cm high by 75cm wide (36in×30in) and the flat panels that fit between them are 90cm×75cm and 90cm×120cm (36in×48in). The common height, which was determined by my own height and the capacity of my vehicle, ensures that the units align horizontally so that a second row fits on top of the first, but the differences in width allow the structure to be extended as required.

Rows of different heights allow you to adjust the staging to suit different performances or different venues, provided the corresponding units in each row are of the same width. Another possibility is to have an irregular mix of sizes; for example, you might make the shadow screen of different dimensions from any of your standard units, provided that you introduce a corresponding base unit with its size adjusted accordingly. The essential requirements are that your pin-hinges should be aligned and you should design and assemble the structure so that its weight is well distributed and it cannot topple over. Stage weights may be used if needed.

**FLEXIBLE STAGING UNITS**

*Flexible staging units can be
combined in a variety of ways to
create stages for all types of puppet
performance, including shadow play.*
RIGHT: *Hinged and single units pack
flat for storage and transportation.*
BELOW: *Four hinged units and two
single sections make up this shadow
theatre.*

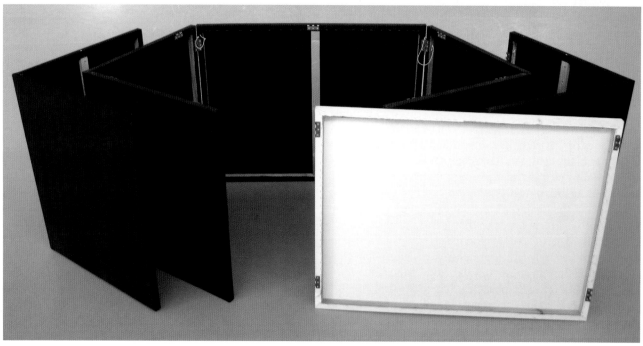

*The shadow screen fits between the black hinged units, but can be replaced by a black unit for use with other types of puppet.*

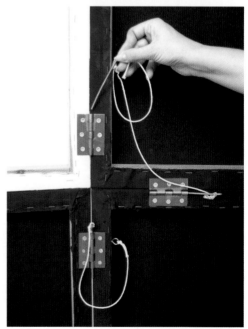

**FLEXIBLE STAGING UNITS** (*continued*)
*TOP: Front view of the units with screen fitted.*
*BELOW LEFT: The theatre need not be flat-fronted; the shape may be modified and alternative sections and screens added as required for different productions.*
*BELOW RIGHT: The staging units are fabric-covered, wooden frames; separate units are joined together by pin-hinges; removing the retaining pins enables the theatre to be dismantled in minutes.*

## Construction

Use 50mm×25mm timber for the frame. Ensure that all joints are true and secure and, if necessary, brace the frame to prevent wobbling. Each section of the frame is made up of four lengths of timber, glued and screwed together with half-lap joints. If carefully cut and secured, they should not need to be braced but, if they do, glue and screw triangular wooden blocks into the corners. Cover the frames before further assembly. Use fabric or painted plywood sheets; I prefer fabric because of the weight and its general appearance, although plywood assists stability. If you use fabric, finely sand all the edges of the frame to avoid any sharp parts that might cut through the fabric with use. Stretch the fabric across one face of the frame and glue and staple it to the reverse face. Take care with the corners and avoid ripping the material or causing too much bulk that will inhibit folding up.

Join two frames together with strong hinges to create the book flats. Use pin-hinges to join the separate units together; align all the pin hinges carefully or the units will not be interchangeable without the need to reset them. To make the pin-hinges yourself, knock the joining rod out of a standard hinge and replace it with a thick, galvanized wire 'pin'. Loop the top of the wire and tie a piece of cord to it; tie the other end of the cord to a screw-eye in the framework so that it cannot be misplaced. Alternatively, use bolts with wing nuts for assembling the stage, but they are fiddly, increase assembly time and get lost; avoid drilling holes where they might weaken the timber and drill them carefully so that the bolts fit cleanly without being loose or too tight.

## FLEXIBLE STAGING IN ALUMINIUM

### Designs

Square-section aluminium tubing presents another type of flexible arrangement. It is strong, light and easily cut

and can be made up into the type of flexible staging units described above or used in single lengths of different sizes that can be joined in a large number of ways. A simple jointing system enables you to dismantle and reassemble it quickly, provided that you have taken care to label all the parts, otherwise it can be a nightmare to sort them all out.

You can use and reuse the tubing and joints endlessly; I have used my set for over thirty years for shadow play, marionettes, glove and rod puppets, open stages, closed booth and proscenium theatre, but I admit that I still prefer the wooden framework where circumstances permit, largely because of simple things such as being able to staple into it or pin something on. With aluminium tubing you need to attach wooden battens to do this. I have used the aluminium set when weight and transport have dictated, such as for air travel, since it can be completely dismantled into a relatively small pack.

### Construction

The flexibility of this method comes from the special corner joints that are available in various orientations, from a basic 'L' shape that joins two pieces of tubing, ranging up to one that will join six tubes, each at right angles to its adjacent tubes. To make a joint, place a plastic insert in the end of the tube, insert the joining piece and tap it firmly into place with a mallet; join the next length of tube in the same way. To dismantle, simply tap them apart.

To reduce a long piece of tubing to a more manageable size, cut it in half and rejoin it with a piece of square-section tube or 'U'-section aluminium, which must be of the same size as the *internal* dimensions of the main tube. Insert half of the joining piece into one of the cut-down tubes and secure it with self-tapping screws; slot the other half of the joining piece into the other cut-down tube. With tubes used vertically, gravity holds them in place; horizontal tubes require a hole to be drilled down through the assembled external and internal tubes for a bolt or some other metal pin to secure the joint.

Attach drapes with fabric tapes or, if they are not too heavy, with Velcro tape glued securely on to the tubing. When using Velcro, remove the curtains from the frame with care; tugging too hard might pull the tape away from the frame. To enable you to secure the shadow screen use self-tapping screws to attach wooden battens all around the relevant parts of the framework. Alternatively, you might construct the main framework in aluminium but insert the screen separately on a wooden frame.

## STAGING CONSTRUCTED FROM SQUARE-SECTION ALUMINIUM TUBING

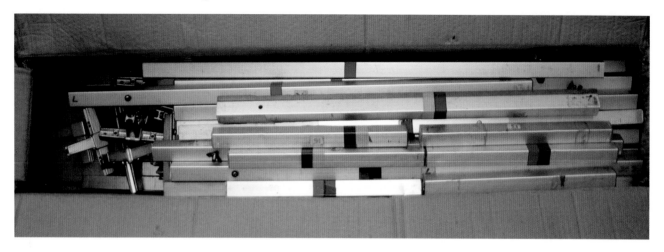

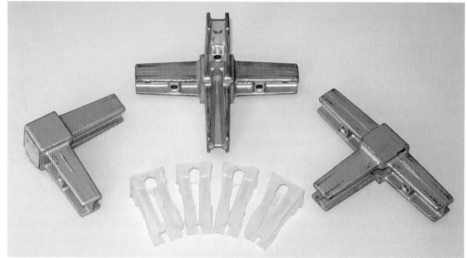

*ABOVE: This box of tubing makes up into all manner of shapes, equivalent in size to the wooden-framed, flexible staging units.*
*LEFT: Corner pieces are used with plastic inserts to join the aluminium tubing.*

*BELOW LEFT AND RIGHT: The plastic insert must be pushed fully into the tubing before inserting the corner piece.*

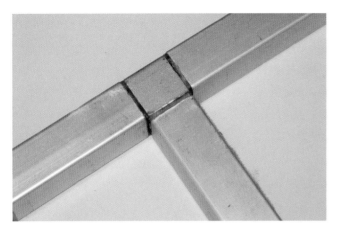

*The corner piece is tapped home fully and provides a strong joint.*

*A four-pronged corner piece is used here to join tubes in two planes; joints are available with from two to six prongs.*

*'U'-section aluminium is used to join and extend the tubing lengthways or vertically; it must have the same external dimensions as the inside of the tubing.*

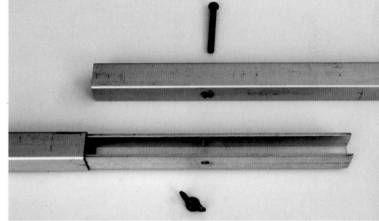

*Half of the 'U'-section aluminium is screwed into one piece of tubing, the other half slots into the second piece of tubing and may be further secured with a wing nut and bolt, if necessary.*

*Wooden battens are screwed on to the aluminium tubing, if necessary, for attaching the screen or curtains.*

121

# 8  SCENERY

## PRINCIPLES

In shadow play, beautiful scenes can be achieved by simple means. Often a mere suggestion will evoke an idea and can be more effective than elaborate scenery. A plain screen with relatively small figures can produce a sense of isolation and coloured lighting on a plain screen can suggest a range of moods or situations.

Whenever scenery is introduced it frequently suggests just a context, partly in keeping with the nature of shadow theatre and largely for practical reasons, because every piece of solid scenery cuts down on the space available in which the puppets can act. It is therefore quite common practice with shadow play to place scenery at the periphery of the screen or to place a single item of it to represent a whole scene or situation or to create atmosphere. Some

*OPPOSITE PAGE:*
*Scenery for Oscar Wilde's* The Happy Prince, *created by Lotte Reiniger for the Hogarth Puppets.*

*THIS PAGE:*
*Scenery from* St Francis of Assisi, *created by Paul Doran, with black card and coloured, self-adhesive film on a large sheet of clear acetate.*

major traditions use no scenery at all. Such scenery as is used therefore tends to be symbolic and its scale does not necessarily relate realistically to the size of the figures.

Sometimes scenery will be highly stylized, showing more than one perspective simultaneously. This is in keeping with traditional Chinese principles, where a setting such as a bridge might be shown partly as front elevation, partly side elevation and partly plan.

## THE SHAPE OF THE SCREEN

The shape of the screen, discussed in the previous chapter, can be a significant element in setting the scene. Within a rectangular screen, a masking shape can be fastened to establish any other shape required. Use a cardboard cut-out, a sheet of three-ply wood, a sheet of coloured translucent acetate or even a piece of fabric, cut and stitched to shape or simply draped. Alternatively, project the required shape by one of the projection methods described in the next chapter (page 145). You can establish any shape, or change it during a performance, without the need to carry large items of scenery. Projection also offers an easy way to

*THIS PAGE:*
**Gilgamesh** *by* **Teatro Gioco Vita,** *Italy.*

*OPPOSITE PAGE:*
*TOP:* **Bold and effective scene-setting by Jessica Souhami.**
*MIDDLE LEFT:* **A lunette-shaped screen.**
*MIDDLE RIGHT:* **An archway-shaped screen.**
*BOTTOM LEFT:* **A circular screen.**
*BOTTOM RIGHT:* **A screen shaped as an open book.**

create textured surfaces or lighting effects across the entire screen. Popular shapes include a lunette, archway or circle, and some performers have used the shape of an open book effectively.

## CONSTRUCTING SCENERY

Shadow puppets often move better if they have a surface upon which to walk, kneel or sit, so add small strips of wood to any scenery that is to support the puppet. The tops of large items of scenery might tend to fall away from the

screen. To prevent this, glue a strip of wood to the back of the scenery to support it. You might also need a strip along the base, joined to the upright with a half-lap joint.

## SOLID AND CUT-OUT SCENERY

Make solid scenes from stiff card of at least the same thickness as that used for the puppets, or use three-ply wood for larger sets. Sometimes a scene is cut within a large black shape so that it appears on the screen as an area of white. Shadow figures are then operated within the white area.

## TRANSLUCENT SETS

Translucent sets permit figures to be visible through the scenery. Take care to ensure sufficient clarity of the figures against the sets so that the picture created is not confusing for the audience and the figures are readily distinguishable. When creating translucent scenery, choose and use any adhesive carefully. Generally, all-purpose clear adhesives such as UHU are satisfactory, but they need to be spread thinly and evenly to avoid unsightly blobs.

## PATTERN, TONE, TEXTURE AND COLOUR IN SCENERY

Possible variations in tone, pattern, texture and colour, described in the chapter on detail, decoration and transformation for shadow puppets (page 67), apply also to scenery, and leaves, grasses, reeds and other natural objects can enhance scenery with their great variations in shape, form, tone and opacity.

## DEPTH IN SCENERY

If you want to achieve a sense of depth in a scene, to structure your sets with the kind of vanishing-point perspective that is used in drawings and paintings is not usually successful. A better solution is to use scenery of different sizes at different heights on the screen or multiple overlays of a translucent material. The use of smaller-scale scenery held or projected higher on the screen is also used to provide another playing level for action in the distance or to accompany linking narrative. You may also use a horizon piece that extends the full width of the screen.

ABOVE: **The Tragic Destiny of a Man of Glass** *by* Compagnie Amoros et Augustin; *figures can appear within solid black scenery by using tightly-shielded or hand-held lights to overlay the larger black image.*

RIGHT: *Jack and the Giant by the beanstalk, by Christopher Leith; scenery and figures are in parchment paper coloured with translucent inks.*

*The use of a horizon-piece helps to give a feeling of depth on the flat shadow screen.*

Multiple overlays produce a variety of intensities of colour or, by using white, shades ranging from white to dark grey. Tissue paper may be used, but it is flimsy and tears easily; greaseproof paper is better and architects' tracing sheet is superior, but you can use anything that does the job. If this type of scenery is to be used for live shadow-play it needs to be sandwiched between two layers of clear acetate for strength and protection. It enables figures to be seen as they move past it, but remember that the action will have the greatest impact if the scenery is designed so that the action takes place against the lighter parts. The edges of the scene will be out of sight so ensure that the ground level is sufficiently deep to be visible.

First draw the scene and shade it in the various depths required; use light and dark shading and fine and coarse hatching to differentiate each layer. Lay translucent paper on top of the sketch and trace over the outlines of the darkest parts. Cut out this shape. Overlay another translucent sheet; trace the darkest areas again together with the next darkest, then cut these out. Continue with successive layers, building up the darker shades. Finally add cut-out card for any solid black areas, including the ground level. If you wish, you can introduce coloured, translucent inserts into the scenery.

To fix the different layers in place, trim the edges of the papers that are out of sight so that they are slightly graduated and run a strip of masking tape along the edge to secure them. Cover the entire scene with a complete translucent sheet as a protective covering.

## HINGED SCENERY

You might need parts of the scenery to move; for example, a door or window may be required to open. Attach the moving part with linen hinges secured with glue. In order to open and close it, tape a short length of galvanized wire to the feature that is to move.

## SECURING SCENERY TO THE SCREEN

There are many ways to hold scenery against the screen. Some performers simply tuck the scenery in between the screen and its frame, if the frame is on the operator's side of the screen, but this is not always satisfactory. Scenery can be suspended on thread, but might have an unwanted tendency to move. Scenery may be attached to a stepped shape in wood or metal that fits into a scenery slot behind the screen or to a wooden block that sits on a ledge below the screen and is secured with a clamp, button magnets, Velcro or swivelling wooden tabs.

If the screen slopes slightly forward at the top it might be sufficient simply to rest scenery such as an acetate sheet against the screen. Paul Doran sometimes uses large

*ABOVE:* **The Adventures of Prince Achmed,** *a silhouette film by Lotte Reiniger; layers of translucent tissue paper and solid card were used to create depth with the figures visible in front of the scenery.*

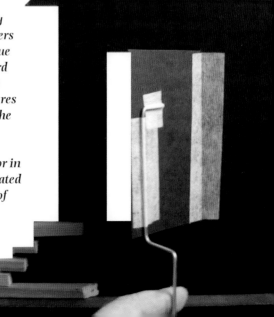

*RIGHT: A hinged door in the scenery is operated by a stepped piece of galvanized wire.*

sheets of acetate that are joined by cords. The cords are threaded through large screw-eyes in the frame of the screen so that, as one scene is lowered from view, another rises into place. The requirements of the performance will call for your inventiveness from time to time. Performers devise scenery on wheels that run in grooves (for example, on curtain rails), scenery hinged to the frame of the screen and swung or lowered into place, or all manner of other devices that are one-off solutions for particular productions.

Whole scenes in their own frames may be set into the frame of the shadow screen. Some shadow theatres are constructed with horizontal, grooved battens above and below the screen. The battens extend beyond the sides of the screen and scenery frames run in the grooves so that one scene can just slide in to replace another or different images can be overlapped. An alternative method has vertical, grooved battens to carry the scenery which is raised or lowered and held in place by wooden pegs that fit into holes in the battens.

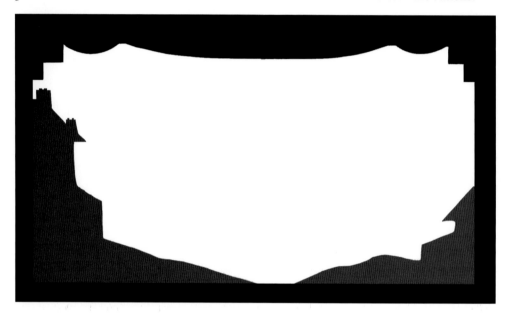

*LEFT: Cardboard scenery in two sections is slotted in between the frame and the screen.*

*BELOW: Holding scenery against the screen; a wooden block sits on the lower crossbar and the attached plywood strip fits into the scenery slot; a strip of stepped-shaped aluminium is a good alternative, or the scenery may be slotted between the screen and the crossbar, and supported by a wooden block.*

*ABOVE: Other ways to hold scenery: a clamp or a swivelling wooden tab secures the scenery to a ledge or directly to the frame.*

*For this shadow show Paul Doran used scenery on two large sheets of acetate, they were joined by cords that ran over large hooks in the top corners of the wooden frame (RIGHT) and lowering one scene caused the other to rise into place; a wooden batten along the base of the acetate sheet prevented flexing.*

131

*A small, cut-out scene is sandwiched between the glasses in a transparency holder.*

## PROJECTED SCENERY

Some materials create different effects depending on whether they are projected or held against the screen. Materials that appear translucent when illuminated against the screen sometimes throw an opaque image when projected, so test possible materials under the appropriate lighting conditions.

### A Slide Projector

When making up 35mm slides for scenery projection use good quality, professional slide-mounts and take care to avoid unwanted marks or dust trapped in the slides as these will spoil the enlarged, projected image. You can create the slides in a variety of ways.

1. Make a small, cut-out scene which is sandwiched within a slide.
2. Draw scenery on to clear, transparent slides using felt pens for projectors, such as those made by Stabilo.
3. Take slide photographs of scenes you have created on card; this sometimes results in a reduction in quality or colour.

*Scenery may be drawn on to a glass slide with felt pens that are designed for use with overhead projectors.*

*This slide photograph leaves space for shadow figures to play and does not conflict with the style of shadow play.*

*RIGHT: Cut-out scenery, here with colour and texture added, can be used directly against the screen or enlarged by using an overhead projector.*
*BELOW: This transparency for an overhead projector was photocopied in black and white from a colour photograph.*
*BOTTOM: The opening scene from Caricature Theatre's* **The Snow Queen;** *the entire scene was created on acetate with black paint and overhead projector pens and mounted in a strong cardboard frame to fit on to an overhead projector.*

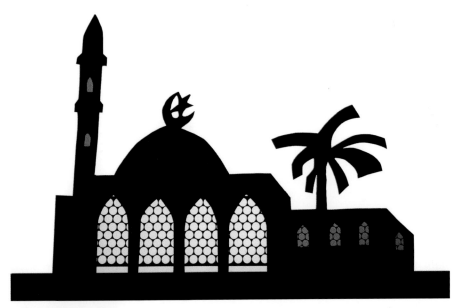

4. Take photographs of natural scenes, but take care that these are in keeping with the style of shadow play.
5. To create abstract images, spread a few drops of glue on coloured glass or place a few drops of coloured, transparent paint on the glass, add a spot of clear glue and mix them together with a suitable implement. You might experiment by adding various types of liquid to paint.

### An Overhead Projector
This enables you to work in a more convenient scale.

1. Create cut-out scenery to place directly on to the overhead projector.
2. Draw or paint scenery (with transparent acrylic paint) on to large, clear transparencies (see pages 70–72).
3. Photocopy images on to a transparency, either in black and white or in colour.
4. Create a collage from solid, translucent, textured and coloured materials and transparent paint on a transparency and allow sufficient material to overlap the surrounding mount so that you can glue and tape it down securely; sandwich the collage between two layers of acetate for durability.
5. Draw or paint an elongated scene on to a long transparency or an acetate roll that fits on to the projector; gently move the strip or wind on the roll to change scene, to create a panning effect or to simulate the characters travelling; a masking frame on the overhead projector enables you to highlight selected

133

PROJECTED SCENERY FROM
CARICATURE THEATRE'S
*THE PHANTOM TOLLBOOTH.*

*OPPOSITE PAGE:*
TOP: *The road was created on
a long strip of acetate for use
with an overhead projector;
the characters walked on the
spot while the scenery moved
behind them.*
MIDDLE AND BOTTOM: *The wooden
frame fits on to an overhead projector and has
an open 'window' between the two plywood
sections to limit the part of the acetate scenery
visible at a given moment. (See also page 146.)*

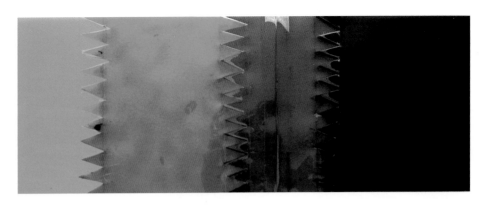

*THIS PAGE:*
*Colour overlays are joined in a zigzag fashion to help to
blend from one colour to the next as the acetate is moved
across an overhead projector.*

parts of the scenery (see the next chapter); the success of this device depends on timing, so practise and, if possible, record and view the results until you are satisfied with the effect.

6. Join separate scenes or colour overlays to move across the projector; create a crisp break or a zigzag joint between each scene or overlap images to blend from one to the next.

## SPECIAL EFFECTS

Effects can occupy another performer and they are not an end in themselves, so use them discriminately. Sometimes effects that are too clever can draw too much attention to themselves. They must enhance, not distract from, the performance. This is another area in which you might be inventive but a few examples are outlined here.

Falling snow requires two projectors directed at the same screen. Use one for the main scene with a tinted background or sky. Make small holes in a long sheet of card (portrait orientation) and place it on the second projector. Draw the holed sheet along steadily to create an overlay of snowfall; this sometimes works better if the snow projector is very slightly out of focus. Also ensure that you pull the card in the right direction!

Similar dual projections are used for effects such as lightning (a jagged cut-out in card), sun, moon and fire. I have seen a piece of frosted glass rotated over red cellophane to simulate flickering flames, but the type and the pattern of the glass are significant for the success of this method.

## MULTIPLE PROJECTIONS

Multiple projections, each suitably masked, were used to excellent effect by the DaSilva Puppet Company for their production of *The Cat That Walked by Himself* (*see* images on pages 105 and 178). A set of Linnebach projectors was set up to focus on a single circular screen that was at least

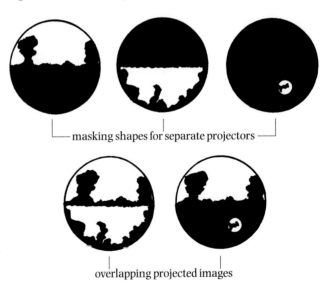

masking shapes for separate projectors

overlapping projected images

*Multiple images can be projected simultaneously but
independently on to the same area of screen; this allows
action to take place in different parts of the screen
without the manipulation of each creating unwanted
shadows on another, it also permits additional
projections within another projected scene.*

*Examples of masking gobos by DHA/Rosco for stage lighting, used to create special effects; the slotted gobo (LEFT) is fixed while the fan shape (RIGHT) rotates, creating the appearance of fireworks shooting out from the centre.*

1.5m (5ft) in diameter. Each projector threw the image of a separate part of the scenery on to the screen. One was completely masked in the lower semi-circle so that only the image in the top half was projected. Another was masked in the upper semi-circle so that only the image in the lower half was shown. This arrangement enabled either one scene or both to be visible at a given moment, fading in and out as required. The figures were projected along with the scenery so that they could be operated in both halves simultaneously without the operators' hands and controls interfering with the images in the bottom half of the screen. The addition of two more projectors yielded a host of possibilities with colour, overlays and so on.

## REPRESENTATION AND ILLUSION

The following chapter contains an example of a rotating ball used for an effect that might represent fireworks, but a long-established visual illusion can be used equally well for this, and for a variety of other purposes too. Years ago the effect was achieved with a light shining through two different cut-out shapes, usually made of stiff card and pivoted together at their central points. One shape was fixed

while the other rotated. The rotating card allowed the light to emerge from different parts of the fixed shape so that it appeared to move outwards from the centre. This can look like a firework or, suitably masked rather than as a full circle, can be used to represent phenomena such as running water, fountains and waterfalls.

Today an alternative to the home-made device is available in the form of masking gobos (*see* page 156) designed for professional lighting units. They are available in a variety of patterns and a gobo rotator is available which fits on the front of a lantern, holding one image still while rotating the other to achieve the same effect as that described above.

## PROPS

Props may have their own controls. However, when a prop needs to be handled by a character, having to move an additional rod in keeping with a figure is not always easy. It may be preferable to have a small strip of Velcro attached to the character's hand and to the object. By pressing the hand to the object a fairly secure attachment is effected, but it will usually not be possible to release the object without using your own hand.

ABOVE: *Cinderella's coach is supported and moved by a control rod made from an umbrella spoke; made by Steve and Chris Clarke for Shadowstring Theatre.*

BELOW: *Paul Doran's strongman, made by Jessica Souhami in coloured and oiled white Ivory Board, has a strip of Velcro on his hand which presses on to another piece on his weights.*

# 9 LIGHTING AND SOUND

## LIGHTING BASICS

Light is the essence of a shadow and the creative use of light opens up a host of possibilities for shadow play. Traditionally, live light was used, produced by oil lamps or candles, and flickering flames seem to give an added, almost mysterious, dimension to the movement of shadow puppets. The whole feel of the acting area, although unevenly illuminated, was much in keeping with the nature of the pieces that were performed, particularly in the east. There are obvious hazards and limitations associated with live light, so electric lighting is usually the choice for shadow play today.

Many traditional-style performances simply required a well-lit screen with even illumination and, generally, a single source of light at any one time to achieve a clean, crisp shadow. Depending on the type of light and the closeness of the figure to the screen, the simultaneous use of two or more lights will often produce a blurred shadow, so some shadow performers still opt for a single source. However, there are times when you might have different acting areas within a screen and require these to be illuminated separately or with different types of lighting, sometimes

carefully shielded so as to avoid overlap, sometimes blended by design.

Recent developments have also shown that the lighting does not have to be a single unit placed immediately behind the screen. You can have multiple lights used sequentially or simultaneously. They can be above, below or behind the screen, to the sides, on the floor, on brackets fixed to the staging, placed on tripods or lighting stands, on lighting rigs built into the staging, even shining away from the screen for some effects. The choice of lighting method contributes to the feel of the performance. Quite apart from the use of coloured filters, certain lights produce a bright, clear, sometimes stark, effect while others create a warm or a soft glow. Some lights give a very white light with a daylight feel, others have a rather yellow or bluish tinge to them. The nature and the scale of the performance will have a major influence on the chosen lighting source(s).

## POSITIONING THE LIGHT

Position your lighting carefully to avoid casting unwanted shadows on the surrounding walls and ceiling as this will

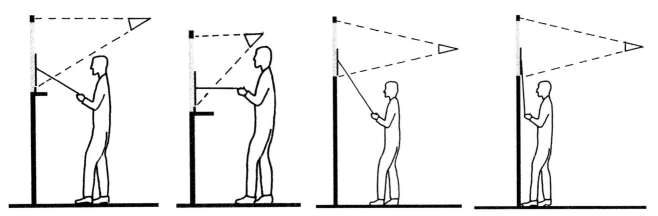

*OPPOSITE PAGE:*
*Multiple PAR38 lights produce a wash of colour over the entire shadow set built for The Lighthouse Children's production of* St Francis of Assisi *at Shadowstring Theatre.*

*THIS PAGE:*
*Arranging the lighting for different operating positions with a larger shadow theatre.*

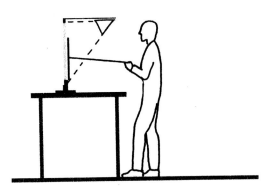

*Positioning the lighting for a table-top shadow stage.*

be distracting for the audience. It is even more important to position the lighting so that it does not dazzle or disturb the audience. With appropriate masking screens, it is comparatively straightforward to avoid shining it directly into the eyes of the audience. It is more difficult to avoid a hot spot, the source of light showing as an intensely bright area on the screen. Even if it is not dazzling, it can be discomforting and certainly distracting for the audience. You can use a frosted Cinemoid or an equivalent filter in front of diffused lighting to help to reduce this effect, but this will not work with more intense lighting sources. For these you need to explore the relative positions of light, screen and audience and perhaps use masks on the lighting. Remember that, if you are to present your production in different places, sightlines for the audience may change.

## SHADOWS AS A BACKGROUND FOR THREE-DIMENSIONAL PUPPETS

When shadow play is used as a background to three-dimensional puppets or live actors, any lighting in front of the screen should be directed so that it does not spill on to the shadow screen and weaken or destroy the images. Remember also that, for shadows to show, the lighting behind the screen must be significantly stronger than that in front of it.

## SAFETY

Ensure that the lighting stands are sturdy and secure and that lamps are not near any inflammable materials. Tape down all leads securely so that they will not impede or trip performers. Regularly check the equipment, wiring, plugs, connections and bulbs. Clean reflectors and lenses and always carry a lens cloth and sufficient spare fuses and bulbs of each type used; also ensure that you have spare, and sufficiently long, extension leads so that they are never straining.

## THE LIGHT SOURCE

Over a range of productions you might find a use for a wide variety of lighting sources. It therefore pays to experiment to see what can be achieved with different forms of lighting used in different ways. Experiment with torches, car lights, domestic lighting, slide and overhead projectors, cine projectors, computerized projections, even candles and sparkler fireworks if circumstances and safety considerations permit.

With soft lighting sources the shadows will disappear quickly if they are moved away from the screen; with hard lighting they will fade more slowly. The use of some types of halogen lamp allows the figures and sets to be placed and move at different distances from the light and the screen with corresponding changes in image size. Some performers prefer halogen lights when creating full-colour images as other types may not give such true colour.

Spread is another factor in lighting. Usually shadow puppeteers want an even intensity of light over the whole screen, a spotlight or other light with a narrow beam can leave dark areas at the edges. Widely spread light, by contrast, looks better on the screen but may need to be masked to avoid excessive 'spill'. The more modest light sources described below enable you to stand behind the screen to operate the figures. The very strong light sources that can project the image require you to operate below the beam of light since they will distort the image if unduly angled.

*ABOVE: In* Gilgamesh *by Teatro Gioco Vita, small figures held close to the screen are in sharper focus, while a projected image covers the entire screen with just a face.*

*ABOVE: A soft 'shadow' created with PAR38 lights by Paul Doran; the owl, from* No Trees No Life, *was made from white card, coloured and oiled.*
*RIGHT: Shadows operated by daylight, with the screen positioned near a window; with diffuse light rather than strong sunlight, the images created are clear while the operators are not visible.*

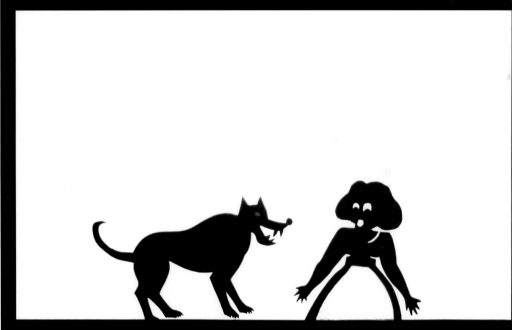

## Daylight

Daylight can create effective shadows but has only limited applications. It is a useful method for educational purposes in a classroom without blackout. Position the screen with the operator's side close to a window to obtain a good, diffused light that provides even illumination and clear shadows, provided that the puppets are held against the screen. The performers' shadows will not normally be cast on the screen unless there is bright sunlight, which might also cast shadows of window frames, change position as the performance progresses or distort the shadows, so careful positioning of the stage would then be necessary.

141

## Domestic Lighting

Some types of domestic light may be adequate for modest forms of shadow-play. As the distance between the lamp and the screen increases, so must the power of the lamp, and frosted or pearl bulbs produce better and more even illumination than clear ones, which can be more glaring and distracting for the audience.

Suspend a light above and behind the screen, but in front of the operators, so as to avoid casting their shadows on to the screen.

Use a reading lamp with a heavy base; place it in a suitable position on a table-top behind the screen, clear of the performer's hands.

Use an adjustable lamp with a clamp and attach it to some part of the framework or to an extension to the stage; a good position is centre top, above and in front of the performer.

## FLUORESCENT STRIPLIGHT

A fluorescent striplight, placed either just below or just above the screen, provides a reasonable, diffuse light, casts no shadows of performers nor of control rods and remains cool. Colour effects with lighting gels are also possible. Fluorescent tubes of between 36 and 70W are inexpensive and available in several lengths. Take care to protect the light during transportation and storage.

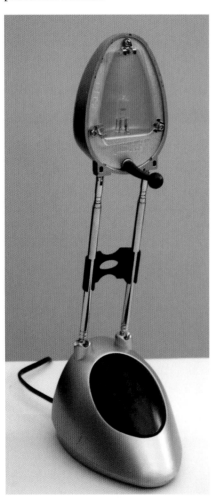

*Domestic lights may be used for modest, table-top presentations.*

*Richard Bradshaw uses a 150W halogen globe (or a 250W softlight globe in the USA), secured on an extension arm approximately 35cm from the top of a metre-wide screen.*

*A fluorescent striplight placed a little way behind the screen provides diffuse lighting without getting too hot.*

The simplest method to mount the light is to set up the fitment behind or just below the screen. Screw the fitment on to a stable base such as a 23cm (9in) wide length of chipboard or MDF (or an old wooden shelf) and attach the fluorescent tube. Place the unit on a table-top or wide shelf behind the screen. Adjust the distance between light and screen so as to maximize the clarity of the shadows. While it is possible to attach the fitment to the framework above the screen, in order to achieve clear shadows it needs to be fixed to a well-supported extension on the stage so that it is held back from the screen.

### Reflector Spotlights and Floodlights

More powerful domestic lighting, such as that used for display purposes or for garden or security lighting, is generally far superior to ordinary light bulbs. Spotlights produce more intense light, but this is usually not as even as that produced by floodlights. Generally avoid bulbs that

*Operating a figure illuminated by a fluorescent striplight.*

*Domestic spotlights and floodlights are useful for basic lighting requirements.*

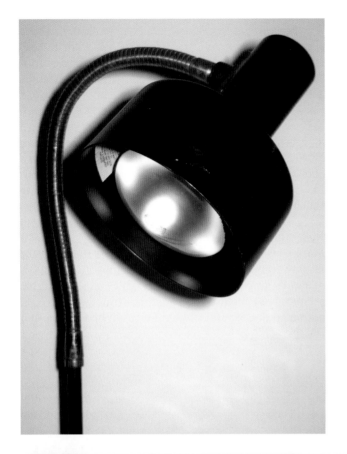

have a very narrow spread of light as these may cause a hot spot in part of the screen while leaving the remainder poorly illuminated.

Most common among such lights is the sealed beam reflector spotlight known as a PAR 38 (parabolic aluminized reflector), which is available clear or in a small range of colours. It provides good lighting for stages of modest size. Clear lights may need improvised holders if you wish to use coloured filters.

*ABOVE LEFT: The flexible end of this lighting stand makes it useful for achieving the best lighting position.*
*ABOVE: A PAR 38 light, a sealed beam reflector spotlight, in an adjustable fitment.*

*LEFT: Paul Doran attached a wooden rack for lighting to the back of this stage; a series of coloured and plain PAR 38 lights are mounted on the rack and may be switched on and off individually or in predetermined pairs or groups.*

Paul Doran (Shadowstring Theatre) has a set of PAR 38 lights mounted on a framework that is attached to one of his shadow screens. A combination of coloured and clear bulbs suitably angled towards the screen and switchable in different combinations produces a splendid range of lighting effects.

Purpose-made light boxes are sometimes used. For flexibility, it is advisable to include a bracket under the box and a hinged one at the rear; this enables the light box to be used for different applications. Include carriers for colour filters and ensure that the box has ventilation slots at the sides.

## PROJECTORS

A projector gives a strong, crisp light and allows for frequent changes of scenery that can fill a large screen. It needs to be square to the screen, unless it is your intention to distort the image. A purpose-built lighting unit with a quartz iodine bulb, technically known as a Linnebach projector (*see* page 150), is excellent for large-scale work. An overhead

projector, preferably with a wide-angle lens, is convenient for creating a variety of images and a slide projector provides a satisfactory light but imposes more constraints than the other methods. Data projectors facilitate the computerized control of any image that may be stored in a computer.

**A PURPOSE-BUILT LIGHT BOX BY GORDON STAIGHT.**
*RIGHT: The light box can hold a variety of types of light, has air vents at the sides and carriers for colour filters.*
*BELOW: A hinged plate at the rear of the light box and an angled plate on the base offer alternative methods of attachment for different purposes.*

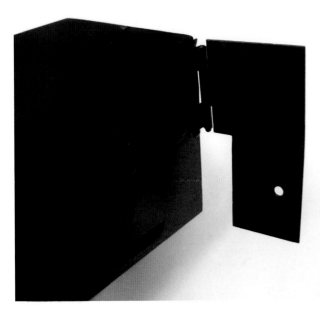

These units enable you to project scenery and effects (*see* pages 132–136) as well as using the light to create shadows of the figures. All projectors will enlarge the image of a figure as it moves closer to the light source, but with an overhead projector you can also lay small figures on to the glass plate and project their images in large scale on the screen.

## Overhead Projectors

When using an overhead projector as a light source, it is often useful to construct a framework to fit over and extend beyond each side of the glass surface. This provides space to position small figures or scenery ready for use and aids the use of long strips of scenery which can pan across the screen.

*An overhead projector.*

**PROJECTED SCENERY BY THE CARICATURE THEATRE.**
*BELOW: The underside of the wooden frame that fits on to the overhead projector to mask the projection area.*
*BOTTOM LEFT: Acetate scenery mounted in a cardboard frame fits into the masking board on the projector; this image was projected approximately 1m wide and nearly 3m high on to a side screen.*
*BOTTOM RIGHT: Scenery for* **The Emperor's New Clothes** *was created on an acetate sheet with black paint and overhead projector pens.*

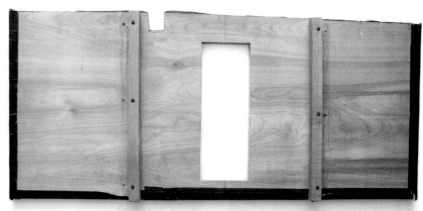

Construct a rectangular wooden frame with cross struts positioned so that the frame fits precisely over the body of the projector. To the top surface of the frame attach plywood (or some other suitable opaque sheet material) to create a projection surface with gaps left for the light to shine through. This forms an effective mask to limit any light spillage. Into the gap fit a sheet of acetate of a suitable thickness to ensure that the entire surface is flush. The acetate also protects the projector glass from becoming permanently scratched. If you are using multiple projectors you might need them to be placed independently of each other, but some applications will require them to play on the same area, for which it is beneficial to have them linked in fixed positions. A useful device for this is a double framework with the cross struts positioned so that the frame fits precisely over the body of each projector, securing them at the required distance apart. Finish the surface of the frame in the same way as the single unit described above.

When using an overhead projector you will usually want to bring the light up steadily and to fade it out rather than to simply switch it on and off. Moreover, if you are using multiple projectors you will usually need some form of lighting control to have a smooth transition between projections or to project images simultaneously with different intensities of light. However, you cannot simply attach a dimmer to each projector or the function of its cooling fan will be compromised when the light is dimmed. You need to rewire the projectors so that the fans work independently of the lighting.

*ABOVE: **This net material was folded to produce a varying density of texture when projected on the screen.**
BELOW: **A textured surface produced by projecting folded bubble-wrap.***

*Patterned glass objects produce various images that can be modified by changing the focus on an overhead projector.*

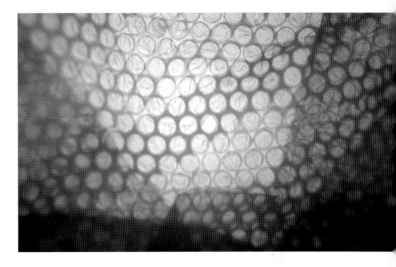

Colour the transparencies with suitable felt pens, glass painting colours or shapes cut from transparent, self-adhesive film. For silhouette effects, use textured materials and cardboard cut-outs or paint on the acetate with quick-drying black enamel. Coloured acetate sheets can be used to cover the entire area and non-naturalistic images can be produced by standing patterned, translucent objects on the projector and by varying the focus. With

*Moiré-type patterns can be created by overlaying the designs on these acetate sheets; the effects change as the top sheet is moved in different directions or rotated.*

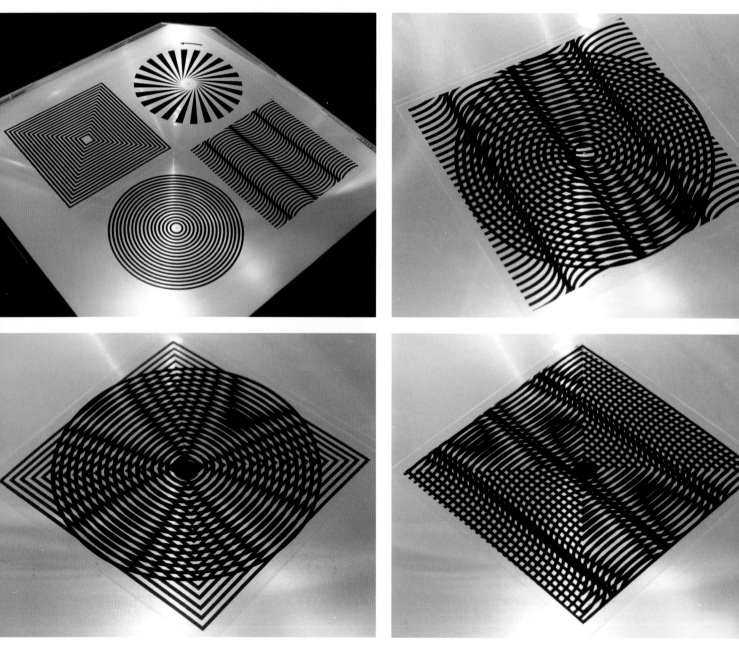

ingenuity, a variety of effects is possible. Mount transparencies in cardboard frames to keep them flat on the projector. Overlaying transparencies enables you to develop or modify any image projected.

Optical-art patterns, or moiré effects, can be used to create a range of changing images as acetate overlays are placed on, and moved over, the basic patterns (*see* Carol Belanger Grafton, *Optical Designs in Motion with Moiré Overlays*, Dover Publications). The technique can be used, for example, to create the appearance of wheels in motion and a host of other optical illusions.

If the projector is not square to the screen, the projected image will be distorted. Placing it central to the screen widthways is not such a problem, but the height of the projector is more significant: if it is too low and projects upwards, the image will be wider at the top than at the bottom, and if it is too high, the image will not reach the bottom of the screen as it is not usually possible to adjust the lens angle below the horizontal, which, in any case, would cause distortion too.

In circumstances where such distortion of an image is unavoidable, you can create a 'distortion grid' to guide you when designing scenery that is deliberately distorted to compensate for this effect. However, this is a difficult process and the amount of distortion the scenery requires will change if the angle of the lens is changed at all. Unless the projector is going to be fixed in a permanent location, I would either ensure that I can adjust the height of the whole unit or use an alternative form of projection.

Constantly changing effects have been achieved by placing on the projector a glass or plastic dish or box containing coloured oils and water and gently tapping the container to create movement. Clearly, liquids and electricity are not a safe combination so this requires either a securely sealed container or the type of projector that has a reflective base plate rather than the more common type with the bulb and electrics below a glass plate.

The standard overhead projector tends to have a noisy cooling fan but there are now alternative models that cool by convection and yet others that work with a reflective base plate rather than having a lamp below, so they need no fan.

## Slide Projectors

Slide projectors are helpful when you have a large number of images and they require little attention during a performance, but, again, their cooling fans can be noisy and, unless you have a wide-angle lens, they need a substantial distance in order to cast a large image. To arrange a smooth change of image or to cause the superimposition of images, use two projectors linked to a dimmer desk with a cross-fade facility. This enables you to dissolve smoothly from one image to the next and to advance a projector to the next image while it is not projecting.

Remember that slide projectors generate a good deal of heat and are not designed to project a single slide for long periods. They are not generally designed for dimming and so the cooling fan must be wired separately from the light. If you intend to project slides, you need to keep the internal parts intact, but, if you intend to use the projector simply as a light source without slides, you might consider removing the optics and have just the halogen lamp as this will give better definition to your shadows.

## Digital Projectors

The availability of digital projectors makes it possible for images to be stored on a computer and projected as required, with timed or manual changes and accompanied by music, speech or sound effects. For this you require the appropriate software on the computer. The speed at which new software is emerging makes it more appropriate for you to seek informed technical advice when you purchase

*A digital projector.*

rather than for me to recommend software that could soon be out of date. Linking the system to a video-editor gives you further control over the projections, which may be composed and changed even during a performance.

## Linnebach Projector

This was developed in 1916 by Adolf Linnebach, technical director of the Munich Opera, as a simple means for background and scenic projection. It has a high intensity lamp with a single, fine filament: the smaller the filament and the brighter the lamp, the sharper the projected images will be. The lamp is mounted in a fairly deep box with a matt black interior and one side open. It has no lens and no reflector. Manufactured versions are usually designed for large-scale theatrical use and take slides of approximately 60cm×60cm or 90cm×120cm. Therefore a purpose-built version such as that described below is better suited to the scale of most shadow play productions. Alternatively, you can create the same effect by removing the lens and reflector from a theatrical lantern of modest size that has a tungsten halogen bulb. Some performers rig up home-made units using a large tin can but I would recommend the construction of a decent unit by someone suitably qualified.

Take care not to look directly into these lamps when illuminated; they will cause discomfort and possibly even damage. If necessary mask the lights appropriately.

### Purpose-built Projection Unit

The cost of a purpose-built Linnebach unit is normally a fraction of that of any of the other projection units described. It is simple and easy to use and, because it needs no cooling fan, it functions silently. It provides a considerable spread of light (for example, up to 4m (13ft) wide) at a comparatively short distance from the screen and so it does not require the same backstage depth as most other projectors. The unit can be used for both shadow play and scenery projection with other types of puppet. By using two purpose-built light boxes side by side, with their bulbs controlled by separate dimmers and with wooden scenery frames, colours and patterns can be blended or dissolved from one to another. The wooden frame can carry a masking shape, cardboard cut-outs, colour gels, clear plastic sheets with designs created with translucent paint, or a combination of these.

The unit consists of a halogen bulb mounted in an aluminium, ventilated light box and connected to the mains via a transformer. I use a 24V/500W quartz iodine bulb but some performers use a 12V/100W bulb. Paint

**A PURPOSE-BUILT LINNEBACH PROJECTOR.**
*TOP LEFT: The light box has a quartz halogen bulb mounted in a bulb holder; note the earth wire at the rear of the box.*
*TOP RIGHT: The light box is mounted at one end of a wooden bar, with the grooved scenery frame at the other end; the entire unit is mounted on a telescopic stand.*
*MIDDLE LEFT: An angle bracket under the light box permits adjustment in any direction.*
*FAR RIGHT: The central bar fits into a bracket which is secured in the telescopic stand by means of a spigot adaptor.*
*BOTTOM LEFT: The scenery frame is attached to the front of the wooden bar by means of a bracket and a wing nut and bolt, so that the tilt can be adjusted as necessary.*

the inside of the box with heat-resistant, matt black paint to prevent reflection.

The scenery frame is a rectangular wooden frame with grooves top and bottom into which you insert cut-out cardboard silhouette scenes or home-made transparencies of scenery. It should have at least two grooves so that you can superimpose images or use scenery together with colour filters. It enables you also to use a manageable-size masking shape for the entire screen, with colour filters or scenery in the adjacent groove. If you insert one scene into a groove already holding scenery, it will smoothly eject the previous scene.

Use brackets with wing nuts and bolts to mount the light box on one end of a wooden, central bar and the scenery frame on the other end. This allows for essential adjustments. Mount the central wooden bar on a telescopic stand by using a 'U'-shaped bracket (mine is made of wood) and a spigot adaptor to fit the top of the stand. When positioning the box and frame on the central bar adjust them so that the edges of the beam fall on to the frame itself and no light spills over the outside of the frame. Make scenery for projection as described for overhead projectors. When cutting out silhouettes from cardboard leave the edge of the sheet as a frame to hold the scenery secure in the wooden grooves. Sometimes I also tape extra items such as dried grasses to the front of the frame.

There are also manufactured Linnebach 'drum projectors', but you might design and create one yourself. This type uses a motorized, continuous loop for the image, for example on acetate. It is arranged so that the loop moves vertically upwards or downwards, creating effects

*A fresnel spotlight by Strand Lighting can be turned into a type of Linnebach projector by removing the lens and the reflector.*

such as the simulation of flames, smoke, mist rising, rain falling and waterfalls.

## Professional Theatre Lantern

These lights usually have carriers to hold coloured filters, gobos (metal masking shapes or effects on glass) or an iris diaphragm with which you can adjust the size of a circular beam. Barn doors (shutters or flaps on the front of the light) give you further ways of shaping or limiting the beam; on some lanterns these are a fixed attachment while on others they are an accessory. When selecting a lantern, check that barn doors and coloured filters or other accessories can be used simultaneously. The weight and the heat of such lights require them to be mounted on a strong fitment clear of drapes or on a professional, telescopic stand.

*Fresnel Spotlight (250–650W)*
Remove the lens and reflector from a modest-sized Fresnel lamp with a halogen bulb to turn it into a form of Linnebach projector. A halogen light up to 500W with a suitable dimmer provides a crisp, clear light.

*Profile Spotlight (250–650W)*
Such a spotlight with lens and reflector intact has also proved to be useful for shadow play. It produces a variable circular beam which, on different models, may be adjusted from approximately 15 to 25 degrees or from 20 to 40 degrees. Built-in shutters are used to change the beam from circular to straight-edged and you can usually sharpen or soften the edges of the beam.

*Mini-floodlight (100–250W)*
This is another possibility. It has a wide-angle, evenly distributed beam and can be used with or without colour filters and barn doors to limit the spread of light. It needs to be at least 1.5m (5ft) away from the area it illuminates.

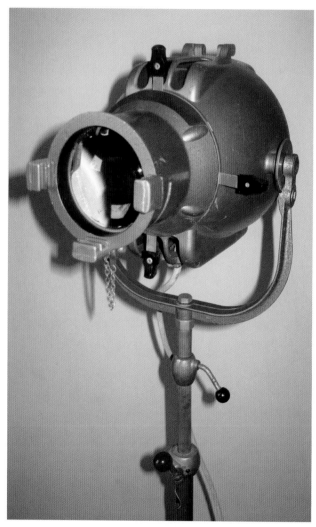

**This profile spotlight by Strand Lighting produces a good light; this model is no longer made but is worth purchasing second-hand.**

*LEFT: A mini-floodlight by Strand Lighting.*
*BELOW AND RIGHT: Shapes drawn on to plastic covers or acetate discs are attached to a torch; the torchlight projects the images on to the screen; this method enables part of the screen to be illuminated while the rest remains dark.*

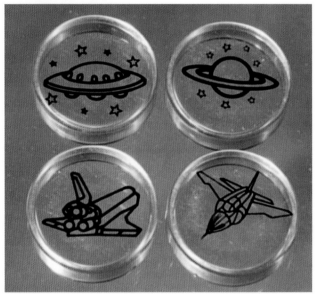

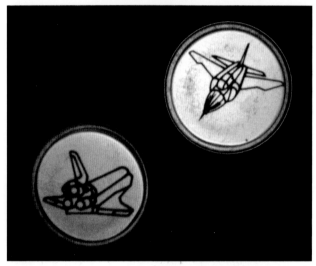

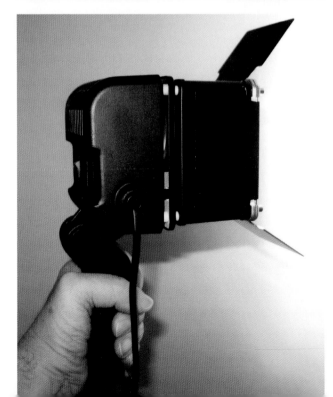

*LEFT: A video-light with a halogen bulb may be mounted on a telescopic stand or hand-held as a portable light.*

## Portable Light

It is often useful to have a light source that can be easily moved and focused on a particular figure or part of the screen. This is usually most flexible if it is hand-held. For some applications a flashlight will suffice, it can be shone on to the surface required or used to project images by placing a drawn acetate shape or cut-out card over the lens. However, this is a very limited device and you will find other types of manufactured or purpose built, hand-held light much more effective.

I have used a video lamp with a pistol grip (with the lens removed) that has shutters to control the spread of the beam. Some companies use a form of home-made, portable Linnebach projector. The device holds a 12V quartz halogen

153

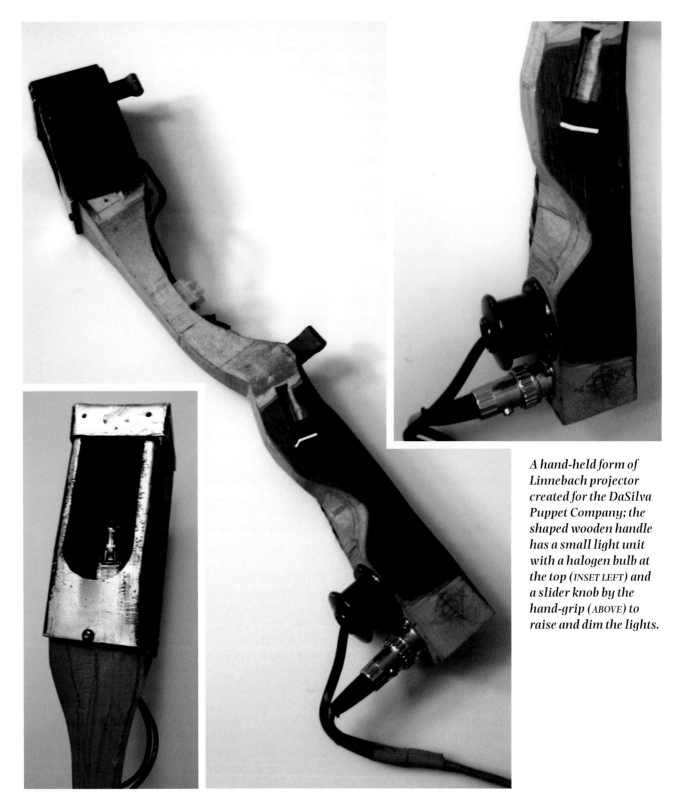

*A hand-held form of Linnebach projector created for the DaSilva Puppet Company; the shaped wooden handle has a small light unit with a halogen bulb at the top (INSET LEFT) and a slider knob by the hand-grip (ABOVE) to raise and dim the lights.*

bulb set in a small aluminium box mounted on a wooden handle. A slider control for dimming is built into the handle for ease of operation.

## COLOUR LIGHTING

Most forms of lighting are plain and require lighting acetates (also called gels) to colour their beams or lights. They are available in a wide range of colours in sheets or pre-cut sizes from theatrical lighting suppliers. You will find that different colour filters change the intensity of the light, and, conversely, if you vary the intensity of the light, it will bring about some variation in colour; even cool colours become warmer as a light is dimmed because the filament becomes redder. The following chapter also contains a description of effects with polarized light which enable you to create a colour change in puppets or sets during a performance.

### Colour with Domestic Spotlights and Floodlights

PAR 38 lights provide a modestly priced source of coloured lighting, as described in the section on reflector spotlights and floodlights (page 143). The range of colours is limited but the use of different combinations of lights and in different intensities gives some flexibility in the effects you can achieve. As the colours are built-in, you do not need separate filters.

### Colour with Fluorescent Lighting

When using colour filters with fluorescent lights the tube usually needs to be completely covered with one or more filters; if any clear light emerges, it will destroy most of the colour on the screen. Fluorescent tubes remain quite cool so some performers simply lay the colour filters direct on to the tube, but this is not recommended. It is much safer and more secure to construct a light box to contain the fitment and its tube and to build runners into the box to hold the filters.

*PAR38 reflector spotlights and floodlights are available in clear and coloured forms and so need no coloured filters; here the bulb holders have been adapted to fit on to the top of copper tubes.*

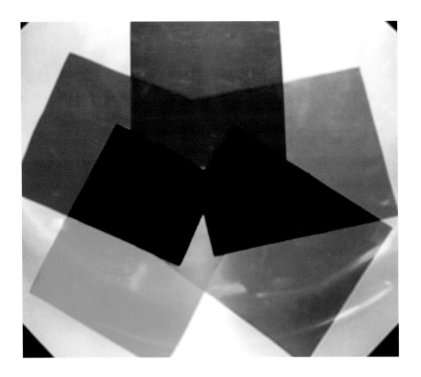

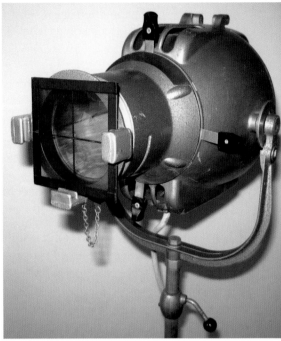

*Coloured lighting gels, here on an overhead projector, can be used with fluorescent tubes, but the colour effect will be lost if any clear lighting emerges.*

*Powerful lanterns require lighting gels to be held in metal frames so that they do not warp.*

## Colour with Overhead Projectors

When you have lights that do not have carriers for filters it is often possible to create your own out of strong cardboard, plywood or metal. For example, there are two alternatives with an overhead projector: either place the gel on the glass plate in a strong cardboard frame or construct a carrier to attach to the bottom of the lens housing, allowing at least 4cm (1½in) space between the gel and the lens because of the heat. Strong card will often be sufficient for this too. Note that you may find a difference between these options in the quality of projected colour.

## Colour with Professional Lighting

Professional lanterns are designed to take coloured filters, but ensure that they are of the heat-resistant type intended for use with such lights. To reduce the possibility of the gels' warping, they should always be framed: the professional lanterns have metal frames for the gels. They are available in different sizes for different lanterns and you might find these useful for other lighting units. The frames can become very hot so it is better to avoid changing then during use if you possibly can, otherwise take great care.

## LIGHTING ACCESSORIES

### Gobos

Gobos are metal or glass masks or filters that are used with professional lighting units. They are available in more than a thousand designs, covering, for example, abstract shapes, graphics and natural phenomena. As well as the standard gobos, they can be cut to your own design in a variety of metals and used to project either a shadow or a light image (*see* also page 136 for the use of gobos for special effects).

### Flicker Wheel or Strobe Effect

While it is possible to use strobe lighting with due warning to the audience before a performance, there is quite a simple way to create this effect. Cut a disc with a combination of closed and open areas and turn it steadily in front of a source of light so that it intermittently obstructs the beam.

The production of *Senor Z* by the company *Amoros et Augustin* included a figure on horseback galloping towards the audience and the effect was just like an old film clip, but a visit backstage revealed that this effect was achieved by

LIGHTING GOBOS BY DHA/ROSCO.

*Metal gobos are available in a wide variety of designs.*

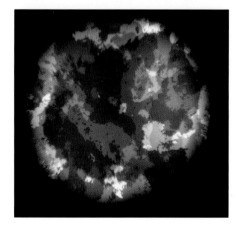

*ABOVE:* '*Colorizer' glass gobos can be used alone for general coloured effects or combined with a metal gobo to create a coloured shape.*
*RIGHT:* '*Prismatics' gobos contain tiny chips of dichroic coloured glass for multi-coloured textures, they produce stunning effects when combined with a metal gobo.*

**Senor Z,** *by* **Amoros et Augustin,** *France; the figures were used with flickering, strobe-like lighting to create a cine-film effect, they were moved away from the screen and closer to the light source to make them appear to approach the audience.*

moving the shadow puppet away from the screen towards the light (so that the increasing size of the image gave the appearance of its coming closer), while the flickering light gave the slightly jerky, and very convincing, appearance of old cine film.

## Novelty Lighting

The children's disco lights illustrated are simply an example of how you might find various pieces of equipment that fulfil a particular purpose. These lights served to suggest colourful fireworks, although I might also have used the illusion described on page 136. Always keep a lookout for novelty lighting with a view to its use for shadow play.

## Telescopic Stands for Lights

Lights of any significant weight are normally mounted on professional telescopic stands; photographic stands are normally too light and topple over too easily. Professional stands are adjustable in height, the range of adjustment being approximately 1.5 to 3.3m (5–11ft) depending on the model. The lantern has a suspension bolt for attaching to a lighting rig; to mount the lantern on a stand you need a spigot adaptor that screws over the bolt and fits into the top of the stand (*see* the images on pages 151 and 152). For stability, telescopic stands have wide bases, so position them carefully to avoid impeding the puppeteers.

*ABOVE*: **Children's toy disco lights were used to suggest a colourful firework display.**
*LEFT*: **Lighting needs to be attached to strong telescopic stands, here by Strand Lighting, suitable for the size and the weight of the lantern; alternatively, they should be attached securely to the staging or to a purpose-built lighting rack.**

## LIGHTING CONTROL

Unless you have a complicated system of lights, you are unlikely to need very sophisticated lighting control. If you are using a microphone, ensure that the dimmers will not cause interference with the sound system as some units cause a slight hum. For a simple means of dimming and raising lights, insert in front of the light either a piece of strong card with a jagged edge or a piece of frosted Perspex.

### Domestic Dimmers

Domestic lighting controls have become more flexible and complex recently so you might use a unit with multiple controls and one master that can dim or raise all the lights. However, you must check that each channel can handle a sufficient load to control the light(s) to which it is connected. Alternatively, there are domestic dimmers with a capacity of up to 650W and these may be useful for shadow play, possibly used with individual lights.

159

LEFT: *A domestic dimmer switch is sufficient for modest applications; it is useful if it has a snap-on or -off switch as well as the dimming facility.*

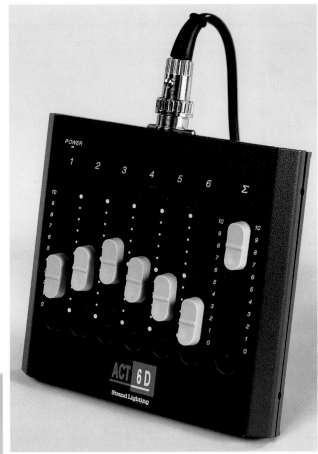

**LIGHTING CONTROL UNITS BY STRAND LIGHTING.**
BELOW: *For larger lights, dimmer packs may be required to handle the load; they may be conveniently placed while the control unit is mounted on the stage.*
RIGHT: *A six-channel control unit with a single, pre-set facility provides handy lighting control via the dimmer packs.*

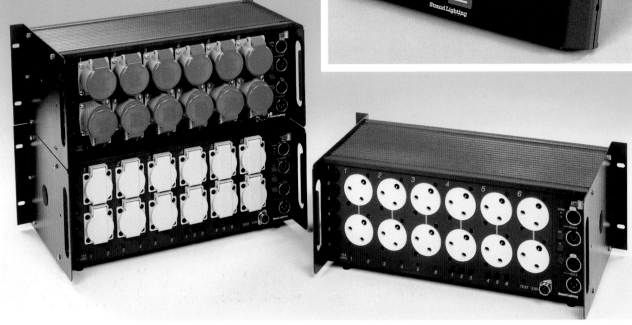

## Medium-range Control Units

Powerful, professional control units generally require large, heavy dimmer packs as well as the control desk, which are too expensive and powerful for most shadow theatres. However, many theatrical lighting companies now produce smaller, compact units intended for schools and amateur uses and these may provide ideal control for shadow theatre.

Some performers are now using laptop computers to program lighting changes with multiple projectors, and the addition of a video editor enables you to compose a range of effects during a performance.

## SOUND

Music is used to create atmosphere, to set the scene, as accompaniment to particular action or as the central theme around which the shadow play is based. Some traditions also make a feature out of background noises, such as the slapping and scraping of the puppets against the screen and the beating of the controls. When choosing music, the scale of the performance and of the puppets are significant factors in deciding what might be appropriate. Long musical themes are rarely appropriate; you will find it more helpful to have music adapted or specially composed for a performance. If the music is copyright, remember that performing rights fees will be payable for public performances.

Live sound has a quality unrivalled by recorded sound, but many small groups may have little choice other than to use recordings for music. However, many of the moderately-priced sound systems currently available offer possibilities for live voices combined with recorded music.

Use the best quality system that you can afford. Most people today would opt to record on to a compact disc rather than a cassette tape because of the sound quality, ease of use and greater reliability. It is advisable to choose a system that enables you to use a compact disc at the same time as a microphone, and that allows for their relative

*A moderately powerful sound unit by Coomber accepts compact discs and cassette tapes, has stereo loudspeakers and inputs for a microphone or radio microphone system.*

volumes to be balanced. A number of microphones need a mixer unit to blend and balance the sources. Choose microphones carefully; there are now many small models that are comfortable to wear as a headset, attached to clothing or on a neck halter. Radio microphones are preferable as they require no trailing leads: they are wired to a small transmitter carried on the belt or hip and a remote receiver is linked to an amplifier.

When testing equipment, remember that what may seem very loud at home or in a shop may be barely audible in a hall, so amplification equipment is usually required, whether integrated or separate. You will probably need separate loudspeakers too, and certainly so if you are to perform in halls because integral speakers are rarely adequate for high volume without distortion. Test speakers for their quality of speech reproduction as well as music.

Do not place loudspeakers behind thick curtains or the sound will be muffled; some performers add a third speaker just below the screen. Check the acoustics from the auditorium and adjust the sound at each venue before a performance. Check also that you do not cause feedback howl from the proximity of microphones to loudspeakers. Wherever possible, plug the sound system into a different electrical outlet from that used for the lighting system. The following sound systems cater for a range of budgets.

### Portable Radio-Compact Disc Player

Larger units (such as 'ghetto blasters') provide quite loud reproduction, even without extension speakers. The volume may well be sufficient for small shows which do not need microphones.

### Compact Disc Player and Amplifier with Loudspeakers

Plug a compact disc player into amplification equipment of the sort available from musical instrument shops. Choose carefully as some are not as satisfactory for voice as they are for music.

### Integrated Sound System

Some manufacturers produce compact, reliable and powerful integrated units for the education market and these are sufficiently sturdy for transporting. Some models have an integral radio-microphone system. Karaoke units are possible alternatives, but cheaper models can rarely compete with the quality and facilities of those designed for the education market.

# 10 CONTEMPORARY EXPLORATIONS

In recent years companies have explored wider possibilities of shadow play using both simple and more complex techniques. A selection of examples is detailed in this chapter. These explorations have given rise to a new wave of shadow theatre companies and productions. New materials, new lighting and presentation techniques may yet emerge and you might find new ways of combining existing materials and methods.

*OPPOSITE PAGE:*
*Astral Angel by Jonathan Hayter, created with translucent collage and acrylic varnish on vacforming PVC, after experimenting with materials; used in the* **Moontime** *production, the puppet becomes the projection surface without the screen.*

## EXPLORING DIFFERENT MATERIALS

Card or acetate folded concertina-fashion enables you to create extending images. You might make the card rectangular, tapered, fan-shaped or irregular, depending on its purpose.

Flexible materials such as fabrics create interesting, flowing shapes. Attach the fabric to control rods or wires or use it for most of the figure, with key parts in a solid material for secure attachments of controls and to give emphasis to the figure.

Plastic materials used for the main parts of a figure enable the image to take on various forms and characteristics by manipulating the periphery.

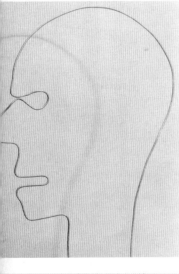

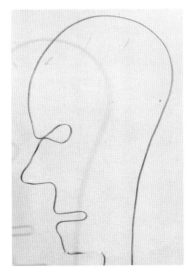

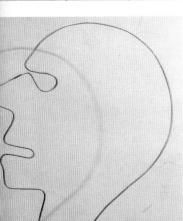

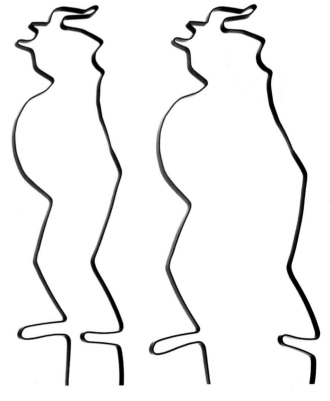

*THIS PAGE:*
*Figures created in wire can transform their appearance and their mood or character.*

*OPPOSITE PAGE:*
*A combination of materials was used for the wolf by*
*Judy Platt for a story within the* Scribble Kids *series*
*by Caricature Theatre.*

*THIS PAGE:*
*Everyday objects, such as this metal 'slinky',*
*can be used to create powerful images as shadows.*

Wire presents a range of possibilities. Different types and gauges have different flexibility, springiness or rigidity and create images with outlines of different strength. A figure may be created from a single piece of wire or a series of interlocked wires. It may be an object, an entire figure or just a face, a hand or a single feature. A range of expressions and moods can be created with a wire head just by moving the two ends of the wire. Materials may be added, if required, to block in parts of a figure or to add colour or texture. These materials may be rigid but will offer greater scope if they are flexible. They must be attached securely to the wire, especially if the figure is to flex, so sewing in addition to gluing is recommended. One way to emphasize any part of the outline is to slip a flexible piece of rubber tubing over the wire.

A combination of materials, both flexible and rigid, offers scope for a variety of movements and effects. A combination, such as an animal with a solid head, rump and legs but a flexible body, creates interesting images since parts of the figure may drift in and out of sharp focus as it flexes or turns.

Everyday objects are used by those who specialize in creating shadow figures or effects with domestic and industrial waste products. They adapt some objects and use others without modification. Some are translucent, others opaque, perhaps with cut-out parts that create pattern or texture on the screen. Their possibilities for creating interesting shadows might not be immediately apparent but it is worth exploring a variety of objects or combinations of them at varying distances from the screen and with fixed lights, hand-held lights and different lighting angles. Combining such images with music can be very powerful.

Paint and oil mixtures create interesting effects too. Dilute paint in water or drop it into some form of oil. Place the mixture between two sheets of transparent film or put it in a sealed plastic bag, such as that used to seal food. Place the film or bag on to an overhead projector to created changing images and colours as the plastic is moved or as heat builds up.

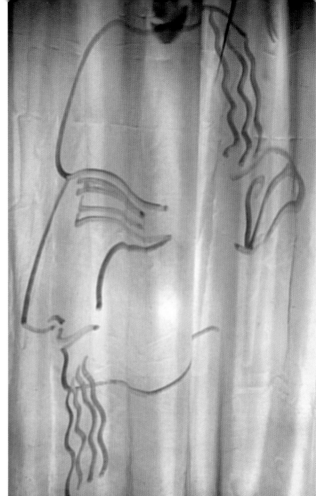

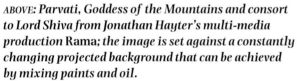

*ABOVE:* *Parvati, Goddess of the Mountains and consort to Lord Shiva from Jonathan Hayter's multi-media production Rama; the image is set against a constantly changing projected background that can be achieved by mixing paints and oil.*

*RIGHT:* *The image was drawn with a felt pen on a glass plate as part of a performance and was projected nearly 2m tall on to the screen, which was made from shower curtain fabric, hung in a slightly gathered fashion; changes to the gathers altered the appearance of the image.*

166

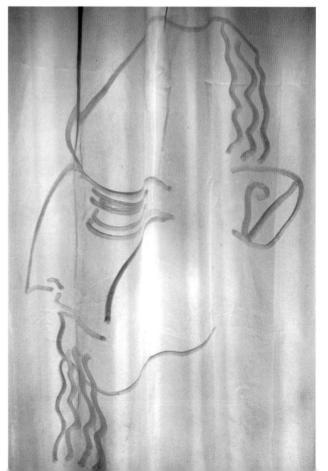

## IMAGES CREATED IN FULL VIEW

Some companies draw images in view of the audience. Project light on to a glass plate that is secured vertically and draw on the plate with a felt-tip pen, paint or beeswax candle. Alternatively, cover the plate with a wash of an opaque material such as oil paint and scratch the image

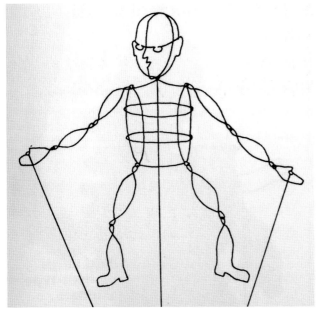

through the paint with a blunt instrument, such as the point of a modelling tool or the end of a paintbrush. Light passing through the glass creates the image on the screen.

## THREE-DIMENSIONAL PUPPETS

Make figures from chicken wire or bend galvanized wire to the required shapes. Join separate parts by interlocking small loops made in the wire. Control the figures with wires operated from below. Solid, three-dimensional puppets with strong designs may be used to good effect to cast two-dimensional shadows; for example, characters may appear at one time as rod puppets and at another simply as shadows. As a three-dimensional puppet cannot be held flat against the screen, a strong source of light, such as a projector, is needed.

Some shadow figures are constructed, not as flat figures but with some curvature or depth to influence the shadows that are created. Translucent or loosely textured materials that can be pleated, draped, crumpled or coiled will appear at different degrees of proximity to the screen and the

LEFT: *A three-dimensional figure constructed with wire.*
BELOW: *The Devil, a slightly three-dimensional figure by Jonathan Hayter, shown first in front of the screen and then behind it with a deliberately blurred image.*

image created will vary as the figure moves. The type of lighting used will determine the extent to which the images on the screen are sharp or deliberately blurred. If necessary, you can create a base shape in clear plastic and add materials to it or attach the materials to rods or wires.

Another related arrangement has proved useful in representing fish swimming or birds flying and may be used for other applications. A series of characters that are either two- or three-dimensional are suspended from a hoop that is itself suspended behind the screen (in appearance like a baby's mobile above a cot). As the hoop is rotated, the suspended figures in the beam of light appear to move across the screen then fade away or leave ghostly images when furthest away from the screen. In this case, it is the figures' relationship to each other that is the three-dimensional feature.

Many years ago, one of my nine-year-old pupils in school created a three-dimensional figure from wire and illuminated it behind the shadow screen with two lights, one with a red lighting gel and the other with green. He made cardboard spectacles, each pair with one red and one green gel in place of lenses. Careful positioning of the lights and the figure resulted in a three-dimensional effect, which was an exciting achievement although with comparatively limited application at the time.

## VARYING SCREEN TENSION

For many years most performers have kept the screen taut with no sags or wrinkles and the majority of performers continue to do this, but more recently some companies have explored other possibilities. There are now taut screens,

*'Man with creatures of the world' from* The Castle of Perseverance *for which* Teatro Gioco Vita *use a somewhat slack screen.*

**FOUR WAYS OF USING A SCREEN** *designed to be longer than the height of the stage, based upon drawings by* Teatro Gioco Vita.
TOP LEFT: *The screen is pulled into a smooth curve.*
TOP RIGHT: *The screen is pulled rearwards and shaken, causing ripples.*
BOTTOM LEFT: *The screen is held loosely and shaken, creating large ripples that may extend towards the audience.*
BOTTOM RIGHT: *The screen is secured at top and bottom while a fan causes it to billow out in a smooth curve.*

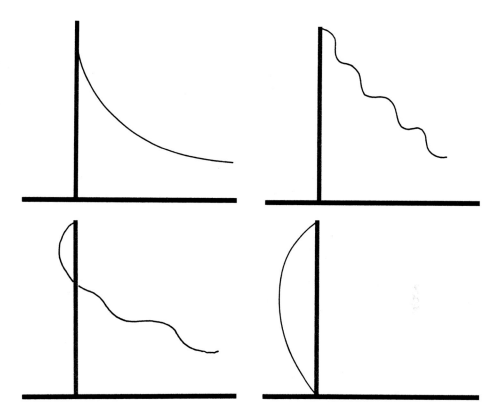

loose screens and screens shaken in a wave-like motion. For example, a screen may hang freely, secured only at the top so that it moves gently in response to currents of air. One production used a screen that consisted of long drapes that reached to the floor and extended further, to be gathered up to form part of the costume of a human dancer in front of the screen. As the dancer moved, the shadow of another dancer was projected on to the drapes from behind, creating a tension between the actor and the shadow.

*Teatro Gioco Vita* achieve a variety of effects with a very large screen that hangs much longer than the height of the playing area and is fixed at the top of the frame:

- with the bottom of the screen pulled rearwards, creating a smooth curve, or it may be gathered at the loose end; or
- the bottom of the screen is pulled rearwards and shaken, causing billowing ripples; or
- the bottom of the screen is held more loosely and shaken at each of the bottom corners to create larger ripples, which may protrude forwards towards the audience; or

- the screen is fixed at the top and bottom but billows out at the centre towards the audience.

So, by pulling, gathering, stretching, twisting, turning and shaking the screen fabric while different lights play on it, the shadows undergo many types of transformation. Add the movement of lights as well and one understands why this is often referred to as *theatre of shadows* rather than shadow puppetry.

## ORIENTATION AND SPACE

Explorations with the shadow screen include the use of multiple screens, not necessarily in a straight line combination but arranged at different angles and in various degrees of proximity, either joined together or separated. Sometimes screens in a variety of shapes are joined together at various angles so that the images are projected through single or multiple screens.

Some performers place the lighting in the auditorium and operate on the audience side of the screen; the audience views the shadows over the performers' shoulders.

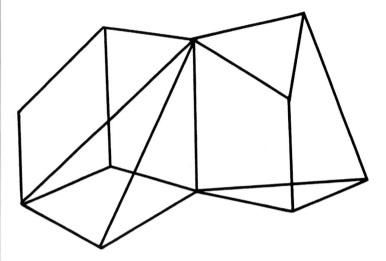

*ABOVE: This framework is designed to be covered by a mixture of translucent screens (sailcloth or shower curtain) and semi-transparent screens (mesh) to create a variety of images on the different surfaces. BELOW: Jonathan Hayter's Light Dancer under two different light sources; the figure is created from vacforming PVC and is partially three-dimensional and becomes the projection surface itself in place of the screen; its surface flickers and alters with the images projected on to it.*

Productions have been concluded on occasions by the performers stepping forward through their paper screen.

The playing space has been altered by hanging curtains all round the auditorium and projecting images on to or through them. The audience is therefore in the centre of the action that happens all around them. Shadows have also been projected directly on to the wall of a building, making use of its architectural features.

Some performers regard the screen as an unnatural barrier, inhibiting contact between the players and the audience. They have therefore adopted other styles of performance. They might play behind the screen, but deliberately show their own shadows as well as those of the puppets. They might play on both sides of the screen, sometimes with actors in front and puppets behind, sometimes with puppet players and actors both in front of the screen. They might use live actors who appear sometimes in shadow behind the screen and then as real people in front of it.

## FIGURES USED AS A PLAYING SURFACE

In a departure from traditional shadow play, Jonathan Hayter (Figure of Speech company) has used figures both as the puppets and as the projection surface by projecting computerized images on to the figures so that, in effect,

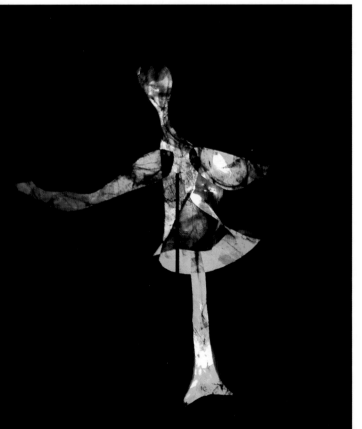

they become a screen. By the use of a video editing desk it is possible to change these images and create new ones even as the performance progresses.

## LIGHT IMAGES

Light images are sometimes introduced into shadow play for ghostly or other supernatural effects. They may be described as the reverse of shadows since you are using masking shapes to create a brightly lit image, rather than a dark one, on the screen.

Bright, reflected images can be created on the shadow screen by using a mirror. Cut out shapes in black paper or card and use double-sided tape or an alternative adhesive to attach these to a mirror to mask the 'neutral' parts you do not want to be reflected. You can create the image in a positive or a negative manner, depending on whether you mask off the features or leave these as the 'active' reflective parts. Alternatively, you may create the neutral section of the mirror or another reflective surface in several ways, with an opaque tape, paint, wax candle or crayons, or any other suitable medium that will prevent reflection. Depending on the nature of the reflective material, you might scratch, file or otherwise roughen parts to achieve the neutral area, leaving the reflective surface clear.

Position a fairly powerful light so that it is directed away from the screen and on to the mirror, which is arranged so that the reflection is projected on to the screen. Ensure that there is no light spillage on to the screen from the lamp; immediately below the screen is often a good position to place the lamp. Shutters that enable you to control the spread of light are useful for directing the light just where you want it to be without casting huge shadows on the surrounding walls or ceiling. Remember that anything reflective on your person or in the backstage area may cast an unwanted image on the screen. Flexible 'safety' mirrors allow you also to distort the reflected images. Some performers use chemical agents or heat these mirrors to change their shapes permanently through bending or pressing the surface.

Note that not all reflective surfaces work equally well. For example, bright, reflective metals, plastics or kitchen foil mounted on card may give an image that suits some purposes but it might be too indistinct for others, although this depends also on the type of lighting used.

Another possibility is to position a light and a mirror as described above and to place a shadow figure or some other object between them. Now the reflected image will

*The Gingerbread Man by Caricature Theatre is used to create a dark shadow, while the sheet of card from which it emerges casts a light image.*

include this shadowy figure. The use of a flexible mirror will allow additional movement or distortion. Sometimes you will want the figure free to move or you can secure it in a predetermined place and manipulate only the mirror. If both the object and the mirror are to move, two operators will be needed to create a single image and they must work with careful coordination.

Sometimes a mirror is placed flat on a table and a light is shone on to the mirror so that the light is reflected on to the screen. Any transparent, translucent or opaque object placed on the mirror appears on the screen in varying degrees of definition. Provided that the mirror has a

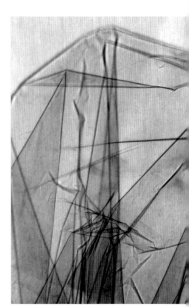

**USE OF A MIRROR TO CREATE REFLECTED IMAGES.**
*LEFT: A strong light was reflected on to the screen by a mirror on which the features were masked.*
*MIDDLE: The reverse effect was achieved by masking the mirror with the shape from which the features had been cut.*
*RIGHT: Folded cellophane was placed flat on a mirror and a light was shone on it to create this reflected image with a varying density of shading.*

frame with a raised edge, droplets or pools of water, paint and oils can be used, with or without images drawn in resistant materials such as candle wax.

Experiment with many types of reflected surface, for example, a mirror ball, to see what images result. Some outcomes will not be useful but the ones that are may prove to be exciting.

Projected light images may be created with shapes cut from card or any other suitable opaque material that can be used as a filter in front of a light to allow only the bright image of the figure to be thrown on to the screen. This method is best used with lighting sources that will not overheat the masking shape, such as a purpose-built projection unit (*see* page 150), an overhead projector, a powerful torch or a suitable hand-held lamp where the mask is not going to be subjected to heat for a significant period.

The chapter on scenery (page 123) shows how to create very small images in inks, paints or a collage of materials inside 35mm transparency slides. For light images you can use a range of media to create the neutral parts of the slide, as described above for light reflected images. For example, you might darken a slide with a lighted candle and then scratch the image from the darkened area.

The same processes can be used with larger acetates on an overhead projector to create a wash over the neutral surface and for different implements to be used to create the positive, reflective areas. Where the nature of the masking sheet permits, you can twist, turn or push it to distort the shape and create interesting moving images. Instead of throwing the image directly on to the screen, its appearance may be altered further by projecting it on to a mirror and reflecting it on to the screen, as described above.

## EXPLORING LIGHTING

Varying the lighting in terms of the lights used or the relative distances of light, object and screen enables you to present a figure or object naturally or to transform its image for your dramatic purpose. These variations can produce changes in the intensity of the colour of an image, change the focus and the size of an image to reveal minute detail, reduce its definition to create a blurred representation or produce a deliberate disintegration of the figure.

The projection of figures placed directly on an overhead projector is possible provided that the puppets are of a suitable size. They are operated flat on the projector and

*Small figures may be placed and manipulated directly on the overhead projector, but they can be tricky to operate.*

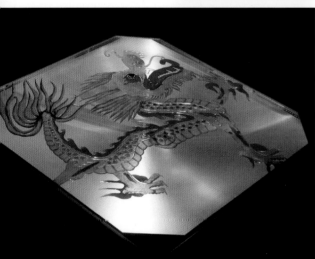

*The Chinese dragon was constructed from hide previously treated to make it translucent and then coloured with dyes; normally used against the screen, for this scene it was projected so that the head was over 1m wide.*

## CHANGING EFFECTS USING POLARIZATION FILTERS.

*THIS PAGE:*
*Clear birefringent plastic, such as a CD cover, without polarization filters (LEFT), between two filters (BELOW LEFT), and with the top filter rotated 90 degrees (BELOW RIGHT).*

*OPPOSITE PAGE:*
*TOP LEFT: Folded cellophane under clear glass on an overhead projector.*
*TOP RIGHT: The same image with two polarization filters, one under the cellophane and one in front of the lens.*
*BOTTOM LEFT: The colour changes as one filter is rotated 45 degrees.*
*BOTTOM RIGHT: The filter is rotated a further 45 degrees to produce another dramatic change in colour.*

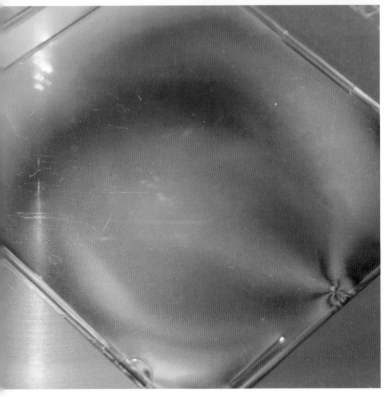

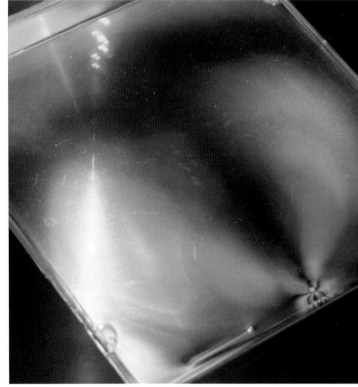

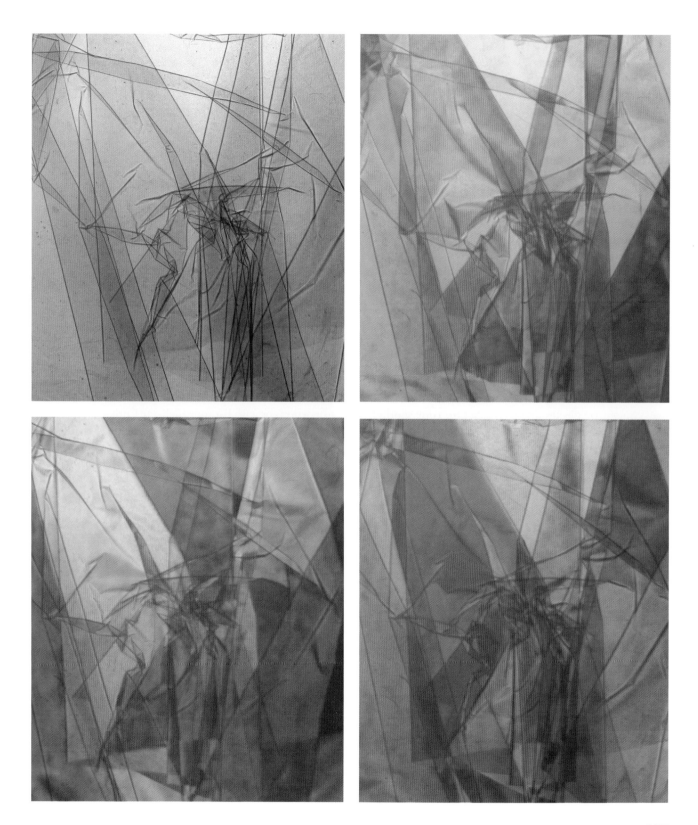

are controlled with thin wire or strips of acetate. However, the size of the figures means that the operator is restricted to very small, delicate movements of the controls so the slightest slip may create gross movements of the figure.

The multiple lighting of an object from different distances can produce multiple images, sometimes overlapping, with varying degrees of size, colour and sharpness. The resultant images will be strong where the shadows overlap and lighter at the periphery, and the images will change as a figure moves. Try moving it at different distances relative to the screen and the light, and turning and tilting the figure can further vary the image through distortion or blurring.

Changing a series of lights from adjacent to well spaced, adjusting the beam horizontally or varying colour filters while modifying the distance of the figure from the screen all contribute to a wide range of resulting images (*see* also using multiple projectors to overlay images, page 135).

Another type of multiple image of a figure or an object may be created on the screen with just a strong spotlight and a sheet of perforated cardboard. Punch a set of small holes in the card fairly close together and equally spaced – you might make them in a pattern such as four by four, five by five, concentric circles and so on. Set up your spotlight and arrange the card a little way in front of it with a space between them. In the space, close to the spotlight, hold the object to be projected, multiple images of the object will appear on the screen. Experiment with relative positions and distances of light, object, card and screen to get appropriate images and to achieve a variety of effects.

The polarization of light enables you to create an unusual colour-change effect in puppets or sets during a performance. The object or scene that is to undergo the change needs to be made from a birefringent material; many plastics are birefringent because their molecules are 'frozen' in a stretched formation during manufacture. A good example is the plastic of a CD jewel case, and cellophane works well too. The object or image may be made from clear acetate or Perspex covered with a coloured material such as cellophane. Place or hold it between two polarization filters while a strong beam of light shines through all three. By rotating one of the filters, the colour of the object will change before your eyes. The second filter may be placed directly on to the object to be projected or, if used with an overhead projector, may be attached in front of the lens.

A lighting rig of the more experimental companies might comprise one or more lighting racks, designed to carry multiple lights of different sorts. For example, they

*OPPOSITE PAGE:*
*The doll is torn apart in Caricature Theatre's production of* The Hapless Child *by Edward Gorey; the production used silent film techniques, accompanied by music, with live actors and a screen approximately 2.5m square.*

might have a floor-mounted lamp, a projector (data, slide, overhead), a halogen light box with scenery frame and an adjustable or moveable lamp all playing at different times – or two sources simultaneously – on to the same screen, different parts of a screen or on to different screens or spaces. They might have two or three identical halogen light boxes in a row. Everything depends on the requirements of the performance, but take care not to use clever devices for their own sake; use what is essential to achieve your objective.

## ACTORS AS SHADOW PLAYERS

A character might appear both as a puppet in different sizes and as an actor, sometimes masked. Costumed or masked actors can have a powerful presence in shadow play, whether with boldly defined masks and exaggerated proportions or with the more delicate human shape.

If you require masks, they may be designed as a full mask to fit over the human head or a flat, cut-out shape may be attached to a headband or skullcap. Design and cut out the shape in stiff cardboard. If you make it larger than the human head you will be able to show the eye that would not normally be seen in the human shadow. Attach it securely to a strip of cardboard that has been made into a band to fit the performer's head which will be hidden by the costume. The suggestion of costume may be achieved through draped fabric; it may be textured, loose and flowing, or stiff and sticking out, as the character requires.

Rather than a complete head, you may create just one exaggerated feature, such as a nose or a beak, and secure this on the actor's head with strong elastic. You might add a head band to which is attached a hat, suitable material to represent hair or whatever is required for the character. The use of cardboard is, of course, just an example. You can use any suitable material and wire offers many possibilities. Whatever material you use, you can also add colour and texture to the character as described previously. The hands may be elaborated by gluing and sewing strips of card, acetates and textured fabrics on to cotton gloves. Any part of the body may be treated similarly by attachments to a piece of clothing or by a simple harness.

# 11 THE PERFORMANCE

## SIZE, STYLE AND AUDIENCE

In considering what and how to perform, it may be of interest to know what the general picture is for shadow theatre. Most companies or groups range in size from one to five members; it is exceptional for companies to be as large as *Teatro Gioco Vita* which has a company of twenty-five, or some Japanese companies that range from ten to thirty members, including technical staff.

Internationally, about one-third of all companies keep to the traditional black shadows on a white screen, while two-thirds now include colour in some form. It is interesting to note, however, that some of the most adventurous, experimental companies tend to use colour selectively and sparingly. Recent surveys have shown that the companies that use shadow play are divided almost equally between those who perform exclusively with shadows and those who create productions with other forms of puppet as well, and only a fifth of companies perform exclusively for adults. The remaining 80 per cent are split fairly evenly between those who perform for mixed audiences and those who perform only for children.

## SUBJECT MATTER FOR SHADOW PLAY

Songs that tell a story, rhymes and fables translate well into shadow play and they tend to be brief and to the point. Stories from religious sources or with spiritual elements have been widely drawn upon too and poems of various kinds can work well. These range from comic verse and

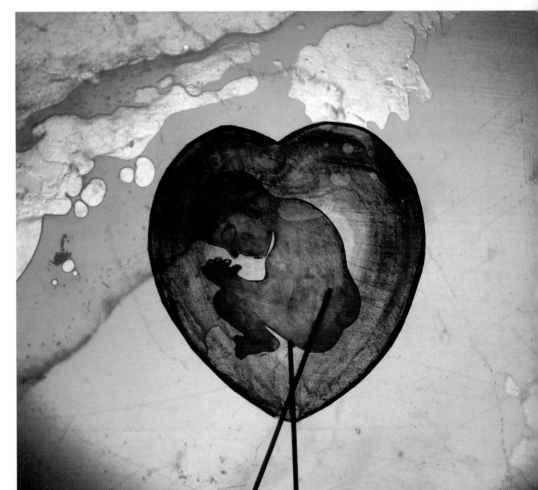

*OPPOSITE PAGE:*
**Rudyard Kipling's The Cat That Walked by Himself,** *designed by Anna Welbourne for the DaSilva Puppet Company.*

*THIS PAGE:*
*Child Born of the Heart, representing the birth of the spiritual self, from* Rama *by Figure of Speech.*

**Tyrannosaurus Rex,** *one of the unlikely animals in a version of 'Old MacDonald's Farm' which gets out of control (Bradshaw's Shadows).*

nonsense poems to works in ballad form; extracts from epic poems, such as the *Odyssey*, the *Iliad*, the *Mahabharata* and the *Ramayana*, have long been adopted by shadow theatre. Some of these might seem daunting propositions, but bear in mind that these sources have many elements and you could take a single episode as your theme.

Popular works by major composers are challenging pieces that provide inspiration for shadow players. Among the favourites are Stravinsky's *The Firebird* and *The Soldier's Tale*, Saint-Saëns' *Carnival of the Animals* and Prokofiev's *Peter and the Wolf*. By contrast, Kipling's *Just So Stories* are ideal for shadow play. Like folk tales and fairy tales, they have survived the test of time and the tales are full of strong imagery. The traditional Turkish and Greek shadow plays provide ample evidence of the adaptability of shadows to

comedy, whether humorous stories such as those of Kipling or political satire.

Although effects should not drive the production, the visual impact of a performance is a major consideration and it is the case that quite a few shadow productions adapt stories that involve transformations. Transformations from solid, black silhouettes to partial or full colour work well and dissolves, enlargements and changes in scale are visually very effective.

When looking at possible material, consider how much of the story can be translated into action. While the human drama is focused more upon language, the puppet drama depends upon action. Remember that, on the shadow screen, even thoughts and memories can take on physical form, literally within a character's head.

Images can change as thoughts change, blending or through superimposition. Two versions of each figure may be presented simultaneously, one remaining static while the other moves to show the thoughts.

The length of the piece must also be considered. Many puppet performances are too long and would benefit from pruning; the shadow puppet, in particular, is not well suited to long performances. Once the attention and the involvement of the audience flag it is difficult to recapture them. A number of short pieces, or perhaps two short plays on each side of a comic piece, usually fare better than one longer play.

Of course, it does not have to be a play. Richard Bradshaw's repertoire includes a series of short items that each has its own 'story'. They are fast-moving, humorous, poignant, some observing human nature, some with social comment, and together they make up a thoroughly enjoyable theatrical experience.

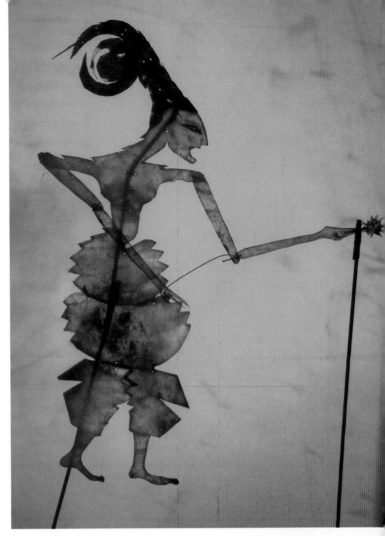

*RIGHT*: *A figure made with painted and scratched acrylic by Jonathan Hayter, after studying Balinese and Javanese imagery.*
*BELOW:* **Machins, Machines et Compagnies** *by* La Citrouille, *France.*

A SELECTION OF ITEMS
BY RICHARD BRADSHAW.
*THIS PAGE:*
*'She was poor but she was honest', a feminist version of the old music hall song; the squire's pointing hand transforms into his head, one of a series of transformations with each chorus.*

*OPPOSITE PAGE:*
*TOP LEFT: The Blaggs, a series of similar figures, transform into an elephant, a woman in a hat, a rabbit and a wolf's head as part of an amusing sketch.*
*TOP RIGHT: The Diver is a typical Bradshaw visual joke, emerging from the barrel as a squashed version.*
*BOTTOM: SuperKangaroo saves the aborigine's hut from demolition.*

*Figures by Jessica Souhami, who took care to research her subjects carefully, including seeking out local community information and involvement.*

## PLANNING A PERFORMANCE

Whatever subject matter you choose, some simplification will often be needed in translating from a story to shadow play, or you might need to select extracts from a musical composition rather than slavishly presenting the entire work.

When you find a suitable story, research the background from which it comes, the culture, the costume, the setting and the historical dimension, if this is applicable. Where appropriate, some performers seek out the relevant local community to look for information, for storytellers and musicians.

If you are writing a play or story yourself, consider the development of character and plot. A good book for children is a useful model of how to construct a story without having a single, simple storyline. In a traditional shadow play you might confine the action to three or four scenes, but the facility to switch between multiple screens means that you can move back and forth between these scenes as necessary, but do not overdo it. The content needs to flow smoothly so avoid long scene changes and long speeches and thus keep the audience interested in what is coming next.

## DIALOGUE AND NARRATIVE

The majority of shadow companies use live voice and music while about a third record the entire performance. Generally, live voice is preferable to a recording because of its nature, its directness and its ability to take account of the audience's responses. If recordings must be used, they should be of high quality. Some performers, including some of the finest shadow players in the world, work without speech and depend entirely on music and mime.

It is not the best use of shadows simply to illustrate a story; often shadow play is most effective when dialogue, and particularly narrative, is used to supplement the picture that the figures present rather than to duplicate what is happening on the screen. The visual picture 'speaks' for itself. Narration supplements this, not by telling you what you can see but what you cannot see; that is, it explains, contextualizes and clarifies that which is not obvious visually, helping the audience to understand what is happening, but letting the images play in their own right.

A narrator usually sits beside or in front of the stage, seldom behind it. Narration is much more than reading aloud, it is itself an art form that must be rehearsed. The narrator must convey the accompaniment expressively but without gestures that will distract from the shadow play. The narrator will need to mark up his/her version of the script with a form of notation that indicates pauses and emphases, rather like a musical score. The narration might include dialogue that will be spoken by the same individual. Some performances use both a narrator and operators who speak any dialogue, but not all operators may have the appropriate voice for the characters and it is not always easy to operate and speak from behind a screen.

## MANIPULATION

To enhance your manipulation, study the movement of people and animals. What are the characteristic features of the movement of a species? What differentiates the movements of individuals within a species? How does movement change with age or with increased weight? How can a particular character convey happiness, sadness, surprise, anger? Explore movements and poses for each character and work with a screen to discover the puppet's

*Two scenes from* Hastings *by* La Citrouille, *France.*

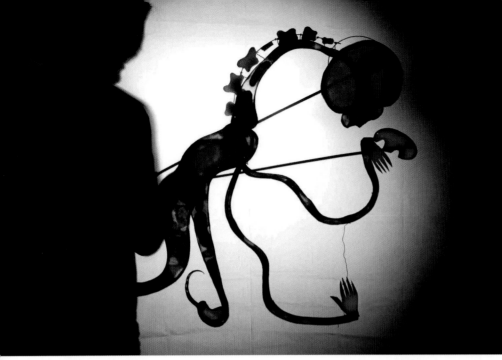

THIS PAGE:
LEFT: *Jonathan Hayter manipulating the Many-Headed Azoth, one of a series of alchemical transformations from* Moontime.
BELOW: *Jack with Clarabelle the Cow from* Jack and the Beanstalk, *by Christopher Leith's Shadow Show.*

OPPOSITE PAGE:
*Paul Doran's spiders, cut from X-ray film, can be crushed without permanent damage.*

possibilities before moving on to rehearse the performance. It may be useful for the performers to act out the piece themselves entirely in mime and to reflect upon their actions, and then to repeat the exercise with the shadow puppets before introducing any narrative or dialogue. This often helps to draw out the character, mood and salient features of the actions that we perform.

Try to achieve contrast, variety and expressive gestures. Aim for movement with the appropriate tempo and rhythm in keeping with the character, but once a gesture is used it is 'spent'. Its effect will be diminished if you keep repeating it, so do not be tempted to overuse a movement with which you are particularly pleased. In the context of shadow play, less is more.

Controls held horizontally or at an angle tend to afford a wider range of movement than those held vertically, and sometimes there is the danger of overdoing the manipulation just because you can, so try not to move the figures too wildly. Aim for economy of movement with clear, precise gestures. Shadow puppets *can* engage in robust action and knockabout comedy, as demonstrated clearly by the traditional Turkish and Greek shadow figures, but be sure that this is what you intend. Do not spoil other types of performance by inappropriate, sloppy manipulation.

Timing and pace are key elements in all types of puppet theatre, none more so than shadow play where timing is potentially a powerful dramatic feature. As in film, the action can be paused for dramatic effect; it can be speeded

up, overlaid or blended, and careful timing with changes of pace and the juxtaposition of images are good strategies for maintaining interest. Some traditional figures, like the Javanese *wayang kulit*, have little inherent movement since only the arms are jointed, but the *dalang* compensates for this by combining arm movements with changes in pace and direction.

Inexperienced performers in particular need to be aware of the tendency to rush the manipulation. Steady, well-paced movements of the figure are often the most effective and the puppets' scale requires that their movements are more deliberate and carefully timed so that the audience can take in the action. Of course, you should not go to the opposite extreme and operate painfully slowly. It is also inappropriate and unconvincing to try to operate a moving mouth to match every syllable of speech, other than for short items where this is a central feature of the piece. It is far better to replace the movements of the mouth with appropriate gestures of the whole figure, sometimes subdued, sometimes expansive, but, at all costs, avoid jerky movements to accompany dialogue. If a character is talking or listening, fine movements or a slight inclination of the head or body will often be sufficient.

Explore the use of space and consider the distance between the figures; this contributes significantly to the visual composition. Furthermore, the action does not have to take place on one level but might happen consecutively or simultaneously on a number of levels. This might be two levels within a structure such as a building or in the foreground and at a distance with the use of a horizon-piece. You can also use puppets of differing size in different positions on the screen, which might enhance the impression of depth.

When seeking to convey the impression of movement towards or away from the foreground, remember that what is involved is more than simply changing the distance of the figure relative to the light and the screen. As with all shadow play, it is about how you execute the movements.

## REHEARSAL

One member of a group may take the role of director or you may video-record the rehearsals and review your performance. First establish the overall movement in the piece – some performers start by running through the entire

*Jean Pierre Lescot, France, used strong black outlines to emphasize the colour and create a bold visual image.*

*Scoundrel and Pooch from* Jack and the Beanstalk, *by Christopher Leith's Shadow Show.*

piece without any discussion or notes. Next, work in increasing detail on individual scenes or episodes within scenes by studying very small units of action. When you are satisfied, reassemble the separate parts, building these up into the whole performance. Rehearse scene changes until they are smooth and not rushed and in keeping with the atmosphere of the performance.

Throughout this process keep a log of the cues, movements, scenery and lighting changes, music and sound effects. Some performers use written notes while others find it useful to have a visual picture with their own shorthand symbols. Plan the backstage choreography as well as the movement of the puppets. The performers need to know not only what they are doing but how this relates to the movements of the other performers.

Arrange figures, props and scenery in the order of their appearance on the screen. Everything should have a fixed position so that it is readily to hand and immediately identifiable in the midst of the performance. Determine where to place the lighting and sound plots, their controls, musical instruments and implements for sound effects.

## FINAL TIPS

Avoid periods of total darkness during the performance. It unsettles an audience, particularly one that includes children. Store figures and sets carefully to prevent damage and prolong their useful life. It is good practice to have cases or portfolios for each group of figures or sets. Do not pack the figures on top of each other but keep each one in a separate 'envelope'. I use cardboard folded and sealed along the side and top to create a sleeve to protect each figure. Before each performance, check the security of all the controls.

Reflect on the performance regularly and review audience reaction. What went well? Were there times when humour did not work or when you sensed that the attention of the audience was flagging? Could it be tightened up in any way? Are there aspects that could be developed to good advantage without making the show too long? Always be prepared to fine tune the performance or even to make major changes, if that is what it needs, and be open to constructive criticism. Your performance will be the better for it.

# 12 SILHOUETTE FILMS

## INTRODUCTION

No book on shadow play would be complete without mentioning silhouette films. The first, feature-length, animated film in the history of the cinema was a silhouette film, *The Adventures of Prince Achmed*, which was based on *The Arabian Nights*. It was created in Berlin between 1923 and 1926 by Lotte Reiniger and directed by her husband Carl Koch. There have been claims of a much earlier film made in Argentina but no evidence of this exists.

This chapter is intended as an introduction to the medium and to provide the reader with sufficient information to

experiment with its possibilities. You will find that silhouette film is one of the simplest and most economical methods for creating animated films. If you wish to take it further, there are many books devoted to animation, such as M. West, *Making an Animated Film* (The Crowood Press, 2005). There is also a great deal of information on the internet if you search key words such as 'silhouette animation' and 'stop motion'; www.wikepedia.com is another such source.

## STOP-MOTION ANIMATION

Stop-motion animation, also referred to as stop-action or stop-frame animation, involves creating a sequence of still pictures that are displayed in such fast succession that the images appear to be moving. These may be drawn, photographic or computer-generated, with two- or three-dimensional animation.

*OPPOSITE PAGE:*
*Papageno from Mozart's* **The Magic Flute,** *a silhouette film by Lotte Reiniger.*

*ABOVE:* **The Adventures of Prince Achmed** *by Lotte Reiniger was the first feature-length, animated film in the history of the cinema.*
*LEFT:* **The Drama in the Park** *by Lotte Reiniger.*

Silhouette film animation is a form of two-dimensional, cut-out animation, similar to that used to create the highly successful *South Park* programmes. However, unlike *South Park* where the cut-out figures are top-lit, the images are back-lit and presented as silhouettes, often with decoration and colour added, as described previously for shadow puppets. At one stage Lotte Reiniger made films in which the figures were coloured on one side rather than plain black. Lit from below, the translucent scenery was in colour and the figures in silhouette, but with top-lighting added the figures appeared in colour too.

Originally, animated silhouette film was created by using a cine-camera with a single-frame mechanism that allowed individual shots to be taken. For *Prince Achmed* Lotte Reiniger took about a quarter of a million photographs and used some eighty thousand of them, projected at 24fps (frames per second).

More recently, video cameras were used by some animators, but the introduction of digital cameras and animation programs for personal computers has created new possibilities for stop-motion animation and made it even more accessible for the would-be animator.

This type of animation is known as 'straightahead' animation because, having planned your sequence, you shoot it frame by frame sequentially, moving your figures a fraction for each frame. You will find two-dimensional computer animation programs that enable you to record key frames (seven for each second of film) with the computer generating the 'in-betweens' (a process known as 'tweening'), but these are for computer-generated images and not suitable for cut-out or silhouette animation which still require you to provide all 24fps.

No doubt programs allowing tweening will emerge in due course for cut-out and silhouette animation too. If they do, approach them with care, for computer-generated in-betweens produce a very different feel that may lack the vitality and the idiosyncrasies that are the essence of straightahead animation.

# THE ANIMATION STUDIO

The room that you use for photographing the images for animation needs to be capable of a complete blackout (a garage may serve the purpose well). It is advisable to cover windows with proper blackout material. Black is best; but especially avoid white blackout material as it will reflect any light inside the room. This will ensure that the work area is completely dark, with the only light being under the figures. Light elsewhere in the room may reveal more than the intended silhouettes (for example, the joints).

The animation studio should have space not only for the animation table but also for additional tables or a work surface on which to rest figures and sets. It is helpful to have a rack near at hand for any tools that you might need without your having to move from the table.

## The Animation Table

The films are made on an animation table, for many years known as a 'trick-table'. Traditionally, the table-top consists of a wooden frame that carries a sheet of glass on which the figures are animated. Lotte Reiniger used crystal glass (transparent plate glass) for its very clear quality. The glass is covered with an opaque but translucent material with lighting placed below the glass and a fixed camera above it. For simple explorations you could use a glass-topped table or a picture frame, suitably supported, with the picture removed. Cover the glass with architect's tracing sheet (or even greaseproof paper). For a better finish, cover the glass with architect's tracing linen or a Permatrace sheet. Alternatively, you could replace the glass with a frosted, acrylic sheet or any suitable plain, opaque, translucent sheet, provided that it is sufficiently thick not to flex while supported only at the edges.

For a more professional approach you should have a sturdy animation bench with space on each side of the playing area to hold figures and long strips of scenery. You may construct this with a timber frame and a plywood surface, but I prefer to use a kitchen work surface (breakfast-bar width) with a rectangle cut from it. It is essential that the table does not wobble, and this might influence how you support it. One method is to support the ends on old kitchen units which, together with the weight of a work surface, provide stability and useful storage space. Another method is to use strong, bolt-on legs of the sort available from DIY stores and firms selling self-assembly furniture, but you still have to provide the stability required and each solution has its limitations. Fixing one long side to a wall will provide stability but will prevent your moving around the table, which is a great disadvantage. Therefore you might fix one end to a wall and keep the other sides clear. Ensure that there is sufficient space on each side of the animation area to accommodate figures or scenery that might be moving to the side of the playing areas.

In order to achieve all-round access, rather than attach any part of the work surface to a wall, you might secure vertical wooden posts with cross-struts extended to attach

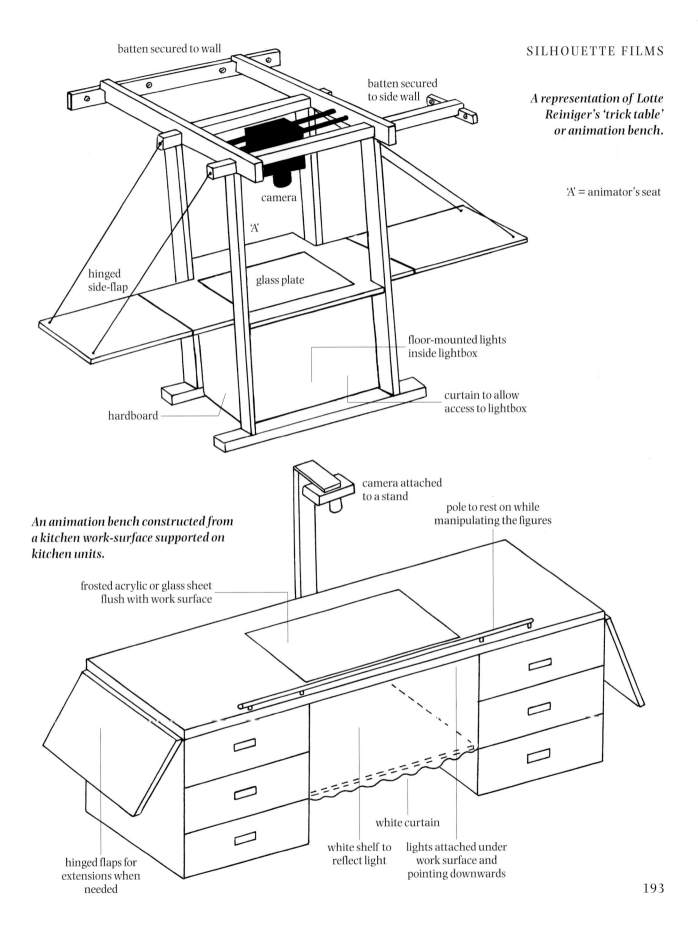

batten secured to wall

batten secured
to side wall

*A representation of Lotte
Reiniger's 'trick table'
or animation bench.*

'A' = animator's seat

camera

'A'

hinged
side-flap

glass plate

floor-mounted lights
inside lightbox

curtain to allow
access to lightbox

hardboard

camera attached
to a stand

pole to rest on while
manipulating the figures

*An animation bench constructed from
a kitchen work-surface supported on
kitchen units.*

frosted acrylic or glass sheet
flush with work surface

hinged flaps for
extensions when
needed

white shelf to
reflect light

white curtain

lights attached under
work surface and
pointing downwards

193

to battens fixed on nearby walls. If you adopt this method ensure that the vertical posts are positioned so that they do not impede your access to the animation area. The height of the table should be such that you can sit comfortably so that you do not have to keep standing up and to avoid backache. An office-style chair with swivel and height adjustment can be very useful.

The housing for the glass plate needs to be rebated so that the glass and its opaque covering material fit snugly and flush with the surface of the table. As an alternative to cutting a rebate, you might position strips and sheets of plywood around the glass and its covering; they must be of the same thickness to create a flush surface.

Another helpful device is a pole supported a few inches above and along the edge of the table on the animator's side. This 'leaning bar' gives you something to rest your arm on while adjusting the position of the figures and thus helps to prevent unintended movements. Also avoid long sleeves with cuffs that might catch the figures.

### The Camera

Expert animators advise you to use the best quality of digital camera that you can afford and this is good advice. However, for your first explorations you will find that a reasonable digital camera enables you to create satisfactory animated films. For example, I first used an old Kodak DC4800 and subsequently a Canon Power Shot G6, both with perfectly acceptable results.

You often need to be able to view the images that the camera is capturing before you take the picture, so a camera with an adjustable viewer that can be twisted is a great asset. If you wish to preview the images in a larger size you can have the camera linked to a desk-top computer or laptop, but it must be positioned so that light does not spill on to the animation table. This also enables you to download the images directly to your computer as you shoot them.

Some sources advise you to select the largest image size you can on the premise that the larger the image the better the quality. However, this might not be appropriate for all types of viewing format, so you need to determine how you intend to distribute your film. Are you going to put it on a website, download it to DVD to share with friends and family, or is it for more professional use? Is it going to be viewed on a computer screen, a television screen or projected? If you plan to show it on a website bear in mind that this will not handle very large files, whereas television or DVD will take larger files. You should therefore determine your image

size in relation to your intended destination(s) and, if necessary, resize the images using a program such as Adobe Photoshop, which provides good quality, resized images.

Fix the camera immediately above the table so that the picture is taken exactly square to the scene. It is essential that the camera support is rigid to avoid any wobble and to withstand an accidental knock. For a first exploration you can use a tripod, but try to arrange it so that the legs do not obstruct your work. There are now tripods with extending arms that allow you to set the camera appropriately, but the tripod should be clamped securely so there is no possibility of its being moved. A better means of holding the camera securely is a manufactured camera stand or your own tubular or wooden rack built on top of the bench with a screw-bracket for mounting cameras.

### Lighting

Whatever type of animation table you adopt, you need a light source under it, directly beneath the glass plate. You might secure a light box to the underside of the table; the inside should be painted white to ensure an even distribution of light. Larger units at floor level need to be screened with any suitable material, white on the inside and black on the outside, to prevent the spillage of light.

The lights themselves do not need to be very powerful and you should avoid those that generate too much heat. If the glass plate becomes too warm, the shadow figures might start to curl. While a number of practitioners describe their lighting arrangements with the lights shining upwards from the floor, I have found that this may give uneven illumination of a larger playing area and so I prefer to have reasonably powered lights shining down on to a white surface to give a broad and even spread of light below the table. With low-level lighting, keep your feet clear so that they do not cause unwanted shadows or uneven lighting.

## PLANNING THE FILM

Before you actually start creating your figures you should have your script and a *storyboard*. The storyboard shows the key points in the animation through a numbered sequence of pictures, rather like a comic strip, with a brief summary of the action represented. Each frame on the storyboard represents a series of shots that make up that element of the film. With this complete you will have a clear picture of what characters, what sizes and what settings are needed for each set of shots, as well as being clear about what each of the figures is required to do.

*Lotte Reiniger's storyboard sketch and the actual scene from* The Marriage of Figaro.

## CREATING THE FIGURES FOR ANIMATION

Figures and sets for silhouette films are constructed in much the same way as shadow puppets, but some important aspects are detailed below.

### Tools

At this stage you will find it helpful to have scissors with fine points, a craft knife, a small hammer, pliers, tin-snips, a roller, fuse-wire and paper fasteners.

### Sizes

The size of the puppets depends on the size of the playing area and the settings in which they are to appear, so it is helpful to have a character in a number of sizes and, indeed, to have a selection of hands in different poses for a single character. For much of the action in a 60cm×45cm (24in×18in) area, like that of Lotte Reiniger, a figure of 23cm (9in) would be used, whereas for distant action it might be 13cm (5in). For close-ups it is preferable to use much larger figures rather than to zoom in with the camera, which should be kept focused on the whole frame. You will also achieve a more detailed finish with larger characters than you would when zooming in on smaller figures.

**The Magic Flute** *by Lotte Reiniger.*

## Joints

Shadow figures for animation usually need to be jointed in a more complex way than shadow puppets for live performance, possibly even with jointed fingers for close-up sequences. Unlike shadow puppets, these figures will not sag under gravity so additional joints are not a problem. The separate parts are joined with fuse wire in a figure of eight on one side and with the ends pressed flat on the other, as described on page 60. Always arrange the fuse wire so that the figure of eight faces the glass and the loose ends face upwards. This allows you to lift the loose ends to open the joint and exchange parts of the figure without disturbing the whole puppet, for example, for a different hand position. For shadow puppets you require the joint to swing loosely, but for silhouette film you need the parts to move smoothly, but not too loosely so as to avoid accidental movement. Therefore, after joining the parts with the wire, you should tap the ends down with a small hammer and then run a roller over the whole figure to ensure that it is flat. If you are weighting the figure, roll it flat after adding the weights.

## Weighting

The separate parts of the figure need a fair weight to ensure that they remain flat on the animation table and that they move only when and as you wish them to. For this reason Lotte Reiniger used to cut some parts of her figures from card and some parts from sheet lead, rolled flat. I have found it sufficient to cut the figures entirely in card and to glue sheet lead on to the card as required, although you must ensure that the lead is not placed where it will obstruct the movement of any other part of the figure. Where a figure is weighted depends partly on the design of it and what it is required to do, but generally you might find it helpful to weight the neck, one forearm, the opposing hand and upper arm, the pelvis, one or both lower legs and both feet.

## FIRST STEPS IN ANIMATION

I did not make my first attempt at shadow film until digital cameras and animation programs for personal computers were available. I had acquired a little knowledge about animation, most of it from a number of demonstrations by Lotte Reiniger many years before and from her writing, but my first try, in very makeshift conditions, brought home to me some of the points that are listed below.

- Suitable blackout is essential for the workspace.

*This set of ten frames represents the 200 that it took to cover the action from the first to the last of these poses; animated digital film by the author.*

- The material used for the screen, its quality and the nature and positioning of the lighting need to be carefully chosen to produce an even illumination without the glare of the light source showing through.
- The work-station must allow you to work in a comfortable position and must be secured rigidly as the slightest jolt can spoil an entire sequence.
- The camera needs to be mounted securely above the screen and its mount should not restrict your access to the figures to move them.
- The size and proportions of the frame (the photographic images) should remain constant.
- Camera settings need to be explored to achieve the best possible images in the conditions under which you are working; the use of automatic exposure settings for the camera can result in unwanted changes in the image, particularly the whiteness of the screen because the areas of light and dark change as the action progresses.
- A high degree of patience and attention to detail are required for film animation.
- A storyboard is vital to establish the key elements of each sequence so that you have a clear idea of the development of the action and can end each action in preparation for the next.
- Great care with continuity is important to create clean movement throughout each sequence.
- To create smooth, flowing animation it is essential to have only the very slightest, almost imperceptible, movement for each frame.
- You need to analyse human and animal movement in order to translate this successfully into film animation.
- There are so many creative and magical possibilities of animation: in this first experiment a ball suddenly appeared in the puppet's hand, as if by magic, yet the film just seemed to flow and the ball's appearance did not break the continuity.
- A more complex, well-articulated figure offers far more scope than one with limited joints that would be perfectly acceptable for live shadow-play.
- Figures are more manageable if weighted to keep them firmly placed and to prevent unwanted movement while moving another part of the figure.
- If 24 frames produce only 1 sec of film (24fps), 1 min requires 1,440 frames and 10 min require 14,400, which means many hours at the animation table

(for convenience, I was working to 25fps, which means 1,500 per min or 15,000 for 10 min).
- When constructing scenery, ensure that the solid base of the set is fairly wide so that the ground level, and therefore the feet of the characters, is always in shot.
- Battens above and below the playing area are useful guides to ensure that the sets are always aligned vertically.
- Arrange the scenery so that important action takes place against the lightest part to enhance its significance and do not let the background distract from the action of the characters.

There were certain matters that I found difficult at first. These were to control movements effectively, making convincing movements, displaying a walking action, having figures pass each other, turn around, approach or recede, transformations, zooming to close-up and panning scenery. Suggestions for dealing with these aspects are detailed below.

### Controlled Movements

You need to move the figures with just your finger tips or the points of a small pair of scissors. Gently push the individual parts of each figure into the position required, keeping them flat on the playing surface. Do not lift a figure to move it as you will break the continuity.

### Convincing Movements

Analyse human and animal movement. Understand the components of each movement. Lotte Reiniger advised, 'You must grasp the rhythm of [a character's] motion, register it in your mind and get the feel of it.' When you animate an animal, 'you must be that animal, moving as it does. The animation will always be stylized but this stylization must be true.'

Timing is even more important in film than in shadow play. Do you know how long it takes to do everyday activities? When planning a movement, try it for yourself and see how long it takes. Of course, you can make changes for effect, but do so with an awareness that will enhance a figure's movement.

### Walking or Running Action

Leg movements seem to flow best if you first move the body very slightly. The legs will follow and almost fall into place for the next frame; then make any final adjustment to the legs. As the figure takes a step forward, every part of the puppet moves so you have to visualize how each part moves in the total scheme of things.

## Figures Passing Each Other
It was difficult at first to arrange for figures to pass one another without any snagging, but this was overcome by keeping one figure still momentarily and covered by a thin sheet of acetate, while the other figure passed it on top of the acetate. The same procedure is useful for separating figures and scenery.

## Turning Around
If a figure needs to turn in the opposite direction you can arrange for this to happen while it is hidden by scenery, but often it will happen in full view. To achieve this, you need different parts of the puppet viewed in different orientations: profile left, frontal, profile right and possibly partly turned left and right.

Place a suitable weight on the figure to prevent unwanted movement and carefully undo the ends of the relevant fuse wire joint(s). Remove the profile shape and replace it with the next stage in the turn. Take the frames required then repeat the procedure until you have completed the turn.

## Figures Approaching or Receding
If a figure needs to approach or recede, create a set of figures graduated in size and replace them for successive frames, moving from just a dot to the largest image or vice versa, as required. You need to consider not only the different sizes but also the progressive movement of the figure and its sequential position on the screen.

## Transformations
For transformations, add and/or remove parts of the figure, step by step until the transformation is complete. To make a character disappear, cut out approximately twenty

**The Magic Flute** *by Lotte Reiniger.*

*The Sorcerer from* **The Adventures of Prince Achmed** *by Lotte Reiniger.*

identical images in layers of translucent paper, with a top layer in card. As you take shots of the image, first remove the card and then successive layers of paper so that the image becomes increasingly faint and finally disappears.

### Zooming in

Avoid using the zoom facility on the camera. It is too fast and too gross for animation. Some people use a camera support that can be raised and lowered a fraction at a time, but I recommend keeping the camera focused on the entire frame and using several sizes of the figure to achieve the zoom effect, with the same technique as approaching and receding characters.

### Panning and Tracking

In panning, the camera moves to show a different part of the scene, while in tracking the camera keeps pace with a figure that is moving across the screen. Having established that the camera is to remain fixed throughout the animation sequence, it is a matter of its appearing to be used in these ways, partly by the movement of the figures but largely by the movement of the background. If you want to create the effect of a figure walking or running some distance, you will need longer stretches of scenery that can be moved along the screen in one direction so that the figure appears to walk in the other. You now have to monitor the movement of the set at a pace appropriate to the action of the figure. The best way to do this would be to have two layers of 'screen' slightly separated so that the scenery can slide along the lower screen while the figure moves on the upper one, which needs to be transparent. It will be of considerable assistance if the bottom of the scenery that is out of shot is marked like a ruler so that the marks can be aligned with measurement markings on the table. This ensures an even and accurate adjustment of the set for each frame.

## ANIMATING THE IMAGES

At a basic level, you can run your images on the kind of software that comes as a package with many personal computers. My first attempts used Animation Shop within JASC Paint Shop Pro, rather than a dedicated movie-making program and you may find that similar software is sufficient for modest explorations. This is useful for trying out 5 to 10sec of animation first, just to see how you get on with the medium.

However, you will find that the size and the number of images that such packages can handle is very limited and you might soon need to move on to a dedicated package. As with all computer hardware and software, new products and facilities appear at a steady rate so, if you decide to pursue silhouette animation after trying out a simple program, explore what software is available and check the minimal requirements for any computer that it is to run on.

Currently, you would be well advised to use a video editor program, which is the best software tool for processing your images for the widest possible destinations (television, computer screen, DVD, CD or web). There are free programs available, but they may allow you to run only 8fps. Adobe Premier is excellent and there is a reasonably priced home video editor version called Adobe Premier Elements (you can download a thirty-day trial version). This program will give you a useful range of tools, such as frame by frame control, an anti-flicker filter, control over the soundtrack and transitions (fading in or out and cross-fading) and enable you to publish your production in a wide range of formats.

Computer programs generally have an 'animation wizard' that takes you though the process quite painlessly, even for a complete novice. To get you started, I have set out in the accompanying box an example of the steps involved in my first attempt at animation on Paint Shop Pro, but remember that this is just a test-level program.

---

**Animating with Paint Shop Pro**

Open the animation program
Open **File** and click on **Animation Wizard**
*Specify the total dimensions of the new animation:*
   same size as the first image frame (this proved to be too large and slowed everything up), *or*
   **Custom size** (e.g., **width 375, height 250, ratio of 1.5:1**)

*Default canvas colour:* **Opaque** (black)
*If a frame has an aspect ratio different from that of the animation, where should it be positioned?* **Centred in the frame**
*How should the rest be filled?* **With the canvas colour**
**[ / ]** Scale frames to fit
[This section should be irrelevant if the camera position and settings remained unchanged because all frames should be identical in size and ratio]

*Do you want the animation to be looped?*
   yes, repeat it indefinitely **[—]**, or
   play it [—] times **[enter number]**

*How long do you want each frame to be displayed (in 0.01sec periods)?* **[4]** (from 1 upwards)

*Specify images to be loaded as frames:*
   click on **Add image** and then **select and highlight the chosen files**
   click on **Open** and the images selected will be copied into the program
The list of frames appears with the option to:
   *add or remove (individual) images*
   *move individual images up or down (change the sequence)*
Click on **Finish** and the animation wizard does the rest for you, saving the animation in a graphics interchange file (*.gif)
Select **View Animation** and enjoy the results

---

These are some further considerations in relation to the animation process.

### Number of Frames per Second

Selecting for how long you want each frame to be displayed determines how many frames are displayed per second of film time. In order to achieve a minimum of 24fps each needs to be displayed for approximately 0.04sec, which will actually produce 25fps. Reducing the display

201

**The Magic Flute** *by Lotte Reiniger.*

time increases the number of frames per second. This reduces the amount of movement required of the figures for each frame and increases significantly the amount of work you have to do to shoot the film, and increasing the display time would reduce the number of frames you need to shoot, but check the number of frames per second required for your destinations. Television and video in Europe (PAL) require 25fps but in North America and Japan (NTSC and ATSC) it is 30. Film requires 24fps. Computer screens require at least 15fps, but I would advise you to experiment to see if this is sufficient for your needs; I prefer to keep it at 24 or 25fps. Even basic animation programs, such as that described above, allow you to specify display times for individual or groups of frames as well as for the whole animation.

### 'Animating on Ones or Twos'

The term 'animating on ones' means using a different image for each frame, while 'animating on twos' means using the same shot for two successive frames. I always animate on ones as this gives a smoother animation. Even though animation on twos is half the amount of work, I have never been as satisfied with the results whenever I have experimented with it. More than two frames per image will not animate well and quicker movements need animation on ones because twos will be too slow.

## Timing

This is something that comes with experience, but you do not want movements to be slow and dreary, nor too quick or the audience will not have time to take in all that is happening. You need to consider the timing of a move in relation to the nature of the action and the speed of the figure and relate this to the number of frames per second. Remember that variations in pace add interest, so you do want some actions that are faster than others, but they should not be rushed. They should always be 'readable'.

At times, you might need to pause briefly on a figure, a piece of scenery or displayed text. This is known as a 'hold' and it is generally considered that a hold needs to be for at least 8 to 10 frames. In the case of words, allow 8 to 10 frames for each word displayed.

## THE SOUNDTRACK

To add a soundtrack you need a basic sound package that will enable you to add voices, sound effects and/or music. A free one to download from the internet is Audacity (http://audacity.sourceforge.net/). Voices are recorded before you start to animate because you need the timing of the speech so that you can plan the frames to match the words.

Sound effects and music are usually added after animation. There are many sources of sound effects on CD that are not copyright, but be aware of copyright on music. Remember also that to record and edit the soundtrack can take a good deal of time.

## IN CONCLUSION

If you decide to try silhouette animation, be assured that it is great fun and the results are very rewarding. My first attempt had a makeshift screen, inadequate lighting, no blackout, an insufficiently jointed figure, no plan of action, a camera on automatic settings and, after taking 200 hurried pictures, my back was aching. But I had 8sec of film looped to run repeatedly. I was pleased with this amateur effort and my two young children were so delighted that they immediately began making plans for their own over-ambitious film. You might like to do the same, but keep it simple and good luck with your productions.

*Mozart's* Don Giovanni *by Lotte Reiniger.*

# USEFUL ADDRESSES AND CONTACTS

There are national and regional groups throughout the world, and also the international puppetry organization, UNIMA. Some are membership organizations which have events for their members but no permanent base you can visit; others have centres with libraries, workshops, exhibits and performances. Some of the centres will have restricted opening times, so always make contact before visiting. Many now have websites and the following organizations will have contact information about other bodies nationally and internationally.

## The Puppet Centre Trust

Established in 1974 as a charitable trust, the Puppet Centre is a national development agency for the art of puppetry. It focuses on contemporary performance practice, encouraging innovation, whilst also respecting and preserving the heritage of the art form. The Trust publishes a web-based magazine, *Animations Online*, and has an extensive reference library housed at The Royal Central School of Speech and Drama in London. (Appointments need to be made at least 24 hours in advance on 020 7559 3942 or 020 7722 8183.)

## The Puppet Centre Trust

Battersea Arts Centre (BAC), Lavender Hill,
London SW11 5TN
Tel: 020 7228 5335
e-mail pct@puppetcentre.org.uk
www.puppetcentre.org.uk
Magazine: www.puppetcentre.org.uk/animations-online

## The Scottish Mask and Puppet Centre

A thriving centre that functions as a building-based arts centre with its own studio theatre, library and multimedia room, display gallery, cafe, mask studio, puppet-making/carving workshops, office complex, car park and grounds. It has a full programme of events and book sales.
8-10 Balcarres Avenue, Kelvindale, Glasgow G12 0QF
Tel: 0141 339 6185
e-mail: info@maskandpuppet.co.uk
www.scottishmaskandpuppetcentre.co.uk or
www.maskandpuppet.co.uk

## British Puppet and Model Theatre Guild

A membership organization founded in 1925, the Guild is one of the oldest existing puppetry organizations in the world. The Guild holds regular meetings across the United Kingdom at which members can exchange views, gain experience through workshops and watch performances.
www.puppetguild.org.uk

## UNIMA British Centre

*L'Union Internationale de la Marionnette* is a non-governmental membership organization and an official partner of UNESCO. Founded in Prague in 1929, it 'unites the puppeteers of the world' to contribute to the development of the art of puppetry. It has national centres in many countries, details of which can be found on the main UNIMA website.
UK membership Secretary: membership@unima.org.uk
www.unima.org

## PuppeteersUK: Puppets Online

A web-based, one-stop source of information about many aspects of puppet theatre, events and performers.
www.puppeteersuk.com

## The International Shadow Theatre Centre (ISZ)

Founded in 1988, the ISZ works on behalf of UNIMA with the objective of conducting and promoting research into contemporary shadow theatre. Its headquarters are in the town of Schwäbisch Gmünd, Germany, which plays host to a major International Shadow Theatre Festival every three years.
Christian Kaiser
International Shadow Theatre Centre, Obere Zeiselbergstrasse 18, D-73525 Schwäbisch Gmünd, Germany
www.schattentheater.de/files/englisch/aktivitaeten/akti vitaeten.php
Shadow Festival:
www.schattentheater.de/files/englisch/festival/festival.php

# Major Contributors

### Richard Bradshaw (Bradshaw's Shadows)

Richard is an internationally renowned solo performer, director and writer, described by Jim Henson as 'a man who produces the funniest shadows in the world'. He has been performing his shadow show for over forty years and has appeared regularly on Australian television for most of this time. A former President of the Australian Centre of UNIMA, Richard has toured worldwide and his show has become a classic in shadow theatre.
7 Mount Road, Bowral, New South Wales 2576, Australia
e-mail: livedodo@hinet.net.au

### Ray and Joan DaSilva (The DaSilva Puppet Company)

Experts in all types of puppet theatre and directors of the DaSilva Puppet Company since 1962, Ray and Joan have toured widely and performed in major theatres, including London's West End. Their company trained many professional puppeteers, sometimes touring three or four teams simultaneously and performing to annual audiences of a quarter of a million. By the mid-1970s they were touring the largest puppet stage in Europe and in 1980 opened the Norwich Puppet Theatre, one of the few permanent puppetry venues in the UK. Now retired from performing, they have a wonderful puppetry archive and their shadow production of *The Cat Who Walked by Himself*, is now performed by their son, Nik Palmer and Sarah Rowland-Barker (Noisy Oyster Theatre Company: www.noisyoyster.co.uk).
58 Shreen Way, Gillingham, Dorset SP8 4HT
Tel/Fax: 01747 835 558
e-mail: ray.dasilva@btconnect.com

### Paul Doran (Shadowstring Theatre)

Paul is an accomplished, award-winning performer, specializing in marionettes and shadows. He currently presents a fast-moving, traditional marionette variety/cabaret style show and is the resident solo puppeteer with a permanent theatre, based at Tropiquaria Wildlife Park.
Tropiquaria Wildlife Park, Washford Cross, Watchet, Somerset TA23 0QB
Tel: 01984 640688
e-mail: paul@shadowstring.co.uk
www.tropiquaria.co.uk/shadow

### Jonathan Hayter (Figure of Speech)

Jonathan is a visual artist and shadow player with extensive experience in performance, intergenerational, educational and multicultural community work. Under the name *Figure of Speech*, he provides workshops and performances in shadow puppetry for schools, theatres, festivals and community groups, with an imaginative range of activities and shows. Now based in Cornwall, he often works in collaboration with artists from other disciplines, such as dance, video, music and animation, to provide engaging and intriguing creative work of a high standard.
Tel: 01209 200853 / 07759 943938
e-mail: jonathanhayter@rocketmail.com
www.figureofspeech.org.uk

### Christopher Leith (Christopher Leith's Shadows)

For many years Christopher has been a leading UK performer, designer, maker, composer, writer and director, an expert in all types of puppet, specialising in marionettes and shadows. A former director of the Little Angel Theatre, London, he has been in demand as a teacher to major companies and theatre courses and has created puppets and productions for many companies, including the National Theatre, the Royal Shakespeare Theatre, the Royal Opera House, the Almeida Theatre and the London Palladium. Health issues now prevent him from performing but he has been documenting and archiving his impressive body of work which will be a wonderful resource for future students of puppet theatre.

### Jane Phillips (Caricature Theatre)

A talented and influential figure in puppet theatre in Britain, Jane is accomplished in a wide range of aspects of puppetry. After art school she trained and worked freelance with many major companies and created and directed Caricature Theatre. Based in Cardiff for nineteen years and performing in Welsh for BBC TV Wales, it was at one time the largest touring company in the UK. Many successful puppeteers today have trained with Caricature Theatre with Jane as their mentor. Now retired from performing, Jane continues to be an active supporter of fellow puppeteers and organizations, and a wonderful source of information.

# INDEX

207